WHAT ALL DADS SHOULD KNOW
DR. JEFFREY SHEARS
DR. CLARENCE SHULER

What All Dads Should Know

WHAT ALL DADS SHOULD KNOW
DR. JEFFREY SHEARS
DR. CLARENCE SHULER

HealthyFamily

"Helping Families Improve & Maintain Their Health"
HealthyFamily Publishing
All Rights Reserved 2011

What All Dads Should Know

What All Dads Should Know is an excellent resource to encourage all fathers and those who assume the responsibility of fathering others. Jeff & Clarence draw upon their life experiences and existing research in a unique way highlighting the special role fathers play in the lives of all children, babies, adolescents, and adults. These authors also demonstrate how critical it is for other loved ones, and men in particular, to support a father along the journey of raising children (broadly defined). Before concluding the book, the authors take special care to view the significance of fathering through a spiritual and religious lens. This book should inspire many to reflect upon their own journeys and find new ways to strengthen their approach to fathering.

Tera R. Hurt, Ph.D.
Assistant Research Scientist
Promoting Strong Families
Program for Strong African American Marriages
University of Georgia, Boyd GSRC

What All Dads Should Know is a much needed book that addresses a modern day epidemic: Absent and disengaged fathers. I especially like the chapter on Fathering Daughters. Shears and Shuler call men to move past their fears and step into the lives of their daughters. If there was ever a time in our nation when our daughters needed daddies, it's today! Read their book and then pass it on to a friend.

Dr. Dennis Rainey
President and CEO
FamilyLife

You need have no prior knowledge about being or becoming a dad to follow Drs. Shears and Shuler's wonderful fathering guide, **What All Dads Should Know**. No matter where you are in your parenting journey, this book will be invaluable to you. I have spent my entire professional lifetime teaching and writing on health and parenting, yet I found myself challenged and informed in every chapter. The man who begins this book with his heart open to becoming a more effective dad will end it with the tools to do so. Few books on fathering will reward a man's labor so richly.

Walt Larimore, MD
Author of 10 Essentials of Happy, Healthy People: Becoming and staying highly healthy

There are lots of "how to manuals" out there. We have them for just about everything. But, none are quite as important, and needed, as ones on fathering. Drs. Shears and Shuler do an excellent job, through personal reflections and poignant observations, of sharing practice advice that good fathers need to be the best dads that they can be. This book is a fantastic resource and one that every dad should keep handy.

Roland C. Warren, President
National Fatherhood Initiative

It is not difficult to be a biological father, but it is extremely difficult to be a successful father. All of us had fathers; some good, some great, some absent, and some abusive. I've never met a man who wanted to be a bad father. Most of us would like to be loving, kind, supportive, and good role models for our children. But most of us need help to make that desire a reality. In, **What All Dads Should Know**, Drs. Shears and Shuler offer such help. The book is readable and practical. I highly recommend it to all fathers.

Gary Chapman, Ph.D.
Author of *The Five Love Languages*
New York Times Best-Selling Author

This book is part memoir from two fascinating men, part "how to" for fathers and part research review. As a daughter, raised by my step father, I greatly appreciate the chapter on filling the gap, and was reminded that I need to tell my dad that he is the best father a girl could ever have. As a mother, I love the message that respecting the mother of your children is essential to loving your child, and that helping the mother models good fathering. Finally, as a person with 21 years on the bench in juvenile justice, I appreciate the research which supports my daily message that children need committed, involved fathers.

Regina Walter, County Court Judge
Fourth Judicial District
State of Colorado

Having spent most of my life working with young people, as a basketball coach for 25 years, most of that at the major college level, and then an athletic administrator for many years on a College campus, the NCAA and later at the Olympics, I have seen up close and personal the powerful impact that fathers have on their sons and daughters both positive and negative as well as the dynamic that the fatherless has on single parent families. This book, **What All Dads Should Know** addresses all of the situations that I have seen and been involved with, especially the fact that regardless of their age or position in life, parents, especially fathers are always the first responders in times of trouble.

Dick Schultz
Former University of Iowa Basketball Head Coach
Former Executive Director of the NCAA & the United States Olympic Committee

Never before has there been a greater need than today for a treatise on fathering on our communities. I'm so grateful that Jeff and Clarence have taken the time to bless me and this generation with this great book. As you read it, allow the Lord to help you become the father you never had, the father you never thought you could be or both.

Dr. B. Courtney McBath, author
Living at the Next Level
www.twitter.com/courtneymcbath
www.crcglobal.org

"Absentee fathers" have become all too common. Men need all the help we can get to understand our God given role and the tremendous potential we have to make a positive impact on our next generation. Dr. Jeff Shears and Dr. Clarence Shuler do a masterful job of identifying the challenges of fathering and then equipping us with timeless tools that will help us father men and women of whom the world can be proud. You will greatly appreciate the practical wisdom and instruction found in this book.

Corwin Anthony
National Director Pro Ministry (Chaplains 4 Pros)
Athletes in Action

I had the great fortune to live next door to Clarence for several years while in Colorado. During this time my wife and I started our own family. Clarence was an invaluable source of parenting for me. Often I would spend hours asking him questions hoping to learn how to father my new family. Seeing his contributions within this book along with Jeff's will hopefully bring as much joy and insight to others as I had gleamed over those precious few years with Clarence."

Dr. Stephen Chadwick
Principal Engineer at Intel Corporation

With two children in their twenties and *one* teen, I quickly realized that they all came *without* an "owner's manual;" *but* through God's greater-grace *I am still in the process of trying to figure it all out.* I have learned over the years that I must bond, build, bend, and believe with my son and both of my daughters in so many creative, unique, and uncomfortable ways. My *roles* seem to shift like the winds as silent expectations of me grow with each passing day —all while no one really knows what I'm thinking and feeling on the inside. It is clear that a dad's journey can be a lonely one but, with **What All Dads Should Know**, Jeff and Clarence *really know what I'm thinking and feeling as a man because they too are journeying as dads.* They have also provided to *All Dads* what I didn't have – the manual, the tool to get it right the first time. So, buckle-up dads *from every race and culture* as we collectively aim to hit our moving target *–fatherhood* and as we reclaim our God intended roles as *lifelong-servants* who are created to "shape lives"!

Dr. Cedrick D. Brown
Former Defensive Back with Philadelphia Eagles; Executive Sales Manager, & Conference Speaker
Sr. Pastor, Commitment Community Church in Lindenwold, NJ
Author, The Racial and Cultural Divide – Are We Still Prejudiced?

Clarence Shuler has written two excellent and practical books for couples. Now Dr. Jeff Shears and he have a new work for dads called, **What All Dads Should Know**. As expected, Jeff and Clarence tackle tough issues with insightful solutions. I know dads will benefit from reading Jeff and Clarence's book and I applaud their leadership in strengthening families.

Ken Canfield, Ph.D.
Director, Center for the Family
Pepperdine University

It was a joy to read this valuable and timely work by Jeff and Clarence. Their topics are engaging and highly relevant, blending good social science research with Biblical wisdom, wrapped in the context of their personal experiences as fathers. Having raised two daughters who are now young adults, I can attest to the soundness of their advice. I could certainly relate to many of the challenges dads have today, especially in the many roles and duties expected of them and have seen first-hand the importance being involved in the lives of my girls. The questions at the end of each chapter can be used as a great resource for engaging men individually or as they challenge each other meeting in small groups. I believe this will be a valuable tool "to turn the hearts of the fathers back to the children. (Luke 1:17).

Richard Leyda, Ph.D.
Professor of Christian Education
Talbot School of Theology,
Biola University

After reading this book and sharing it with a friend one thing came to mind, if all the "Head" of the families were thinking in righteous unison what a different and glorious world this would be. This book if nothing else puts a man in the right frame of mind to accomplish the goal of being a positive and effective role model not only for his children but for other men as well. This is a book that all men should read whether they are Fathers, soon to be Fathers or young men just needing direction to live a positive life.

1SG Brown, Walter T.
U.S. Army, Schofield Barracks, Hawaii
Author, *Advancing the Kingdom*

Through their collective efforts, Dr. Shears and Dr. Shuler have developed a phenomenal resource on Fatherhood that is desperately needed globally. They've provided relational insight on how to become great fathers - something that is long overdue. My prayer is that every dad, both biological and surrogate, will read this book and improve the lives of children & families worldwide.

Garry James, D. Min.
Author of Drying Silent Tears

Drs. Shears and Shuler lay out the blueprint for every father and father to be in ***What All Dads Should Know***. Their combined wisdom, personal and clinical experiences are evident in this incredible resource guide for fathers. Men, who are willing to admit that they need help to be a better father, will get the help, insight and guidance they need from this book. I spend a lot of time working with men and couples and I look forward to pointing them in the direction of this book. After reading this book, you will be a different man, a better man and a better father. Read it, study it, live it and give it to another father.

George James, LMFT
President and CEO of George Talks LLC
Therapist, Speaker, Consultant & Life Coach
www.GeorgeTalks.com / Twitter: @GeorgeTalksLLC

This book brings to life the importance of fathering in today's contemporary society when fathers need to be saluted. It is SO important for our sons, daughters and our families.

Suzanne Mayo-Theus, M.A.,
Assistant Professor
Child Development and Family Studies
Southern University at New Orleans
 Doctoral Candidate, School of Family Studies and Human Services, Kansas State University

Thank you, Jeff and Clarence for your willingness to write a book on fathering with a father's perspective of his impact on his family. As father of adult children, this book helps me understand that my job as parent and father is not over. This book helped me revisit the impact of a father: what a father brings to the table and that it is a job that nobody can do but him. As fathers, we may be the most celebrated person to our kids, but we know that we can lay down the foundation that can positively affect them for the rest of their lives. I have an awesome job and responsibility to guide my adult children in life and this book gives fathers some great tools to help us. As a stepfather, this book gave some great insight on what that looks like and how it is walked out. Great read and again thanks Jeff and Clarence.

Roger Banner, Owner
Kingdom Builders Car Solutions
Winston-Salem, NC

A must read for any man who desires to leave a legacy, impact a life or change the world *ONE CHILD at a TIME!* This is the book to assist you in doing that.

Robert Johnson
Civil Engineer/Logistic Coordinator
South Carolina Dept. of Transportation

PREFACE

My friend -- whom I'll call "James" -- is a CEO, in his fifties. His son, in his mid-twenties, returned from Afghanistan a while back, and has struggled with Post-Traumatic Stress. As he tried to adjust, he started drinking and getting into other destructive habits. Last I heard, he was locked up. So here's James, who's successful and has just about everything he wants, and suddenly his son is in a tough situation.

James told me what happened just a few days before the son went into jail. The young man pulled up into the driveway late one night, and he'd been drinking. He got out of the car, dropped to his knees, and started crying. He knew he was in trouble because of some drug-related issues. And he said, "Dad, you've always tried to fix it and to tell me what to do. But I just want you to be Dad. *Just be my Dad.*"

So James knelt down with his son and started crying with him, and that was a big breakthrough for both of them. Even though the son is in jail, their relationship is on the road back. They're getting to know each other again. James said, "I am just being his dad. I'm not judging him."

For my friend, it took more than twenty-five years with his son to figure out what kind of father his son really needed him to be.

How about you, dad? How's your connection with your kids? That's ultimately what each father needs to ask himself, and that's how this book can help you. Once you have taken in and begun to process **What All Dads Should Know** put that knowledge into action. Follow through on your good intentions. And please hear those words from James' son as if they're spoken by your own child: "*I just want you to be Dad.*" Be that kind of dad for your kids.

One of the things I am proud of in my role at the National Center for Fathering is that we have the footnotes and bibliography. Thanks in large part to my predecessor, Dr. Ken Canfield, our information is based on solid research on fatherhood. And that's one great feature of this book: Dr. Shears has done his homework. He uses research findings to guide and to add further credibility to his message -- and you can reap the benefits.

I want to encourage you as you strive to become a better dad. You're facing real-life family issues that are much more complex than they were a generation ago. Sometimes the challenges dads face are overwhelming, bringing on gut-wrenching emotions: divorced dads who can't see their kids, fathers who have lost their brides to death, dads who are still trying to overcome horrific childhood situations, and the list goes on. It blows me away to hear the stories, and I'm excited about the way Jeff and Clarence touch on many of those issues in this book.

No one would wish for those kinds of challenges; the last thing we want is to be tested by some fiery ordeal. And this may not be easy for you to hear, but those hard times can have a bigger purpose, to shape us and help us develop perseverance and wisdom. It often leads us to deeper relationships and a deeper understanding of trials so that we're better equipped to help other people who have those challenges.

So don't worry if you aren't a perfect father. Welcome to the club! We're all learning and growing, and as you take steps along your fathering journey, please remember -- the test of a great dad is not in your area of comfort, but how you function when your child isn't doing well, when crises hit, when bad stuff happens.

Fatherhood is a special and sacred calling, but it's very much within your reach. If you're prepared and if you depend on God, you can shine during those hard times. Your family needs you to be courageous no matter what might come your way.

As I learned from watching my Pop, succeeding in this role starts with being faithful during the everyday events. You don't need an important title or a bunch of impressive letters after your name. It's not about being "spectacular" or making headlines or starring in the top video on YouTube. You just have to be yourself and be there. *Just be dad.* Simply making time for your kids is a great place to start. Your commitment to your kids can be exceptional, but if you're just taking care of the basics, that's really what your children need most.

Carey Casey
CEO, National Center for Fathering / fathers.com

HealthyFamily

"Helping Families Improve & Maintain Their Health"
HealthyFamily Publishing
All Rights Reserved 2011

Special Thanks

Jeff's Special Thanks: This book would not be possible without my three wonderful daughters, Jordan, Jiera, & Jadah, who have taught me so much. I am proud to be their father. I am eternally indebted to my wife Danni, for her support and allowing me to father my girls. I am thankful to my deceased grandfathers, W.C. Foster and Sam Shears whose everlasting legacy was that they took their families to church to worship with them on Sundays. Most importantly, I am thankful to my father Arlie Shears, who I have simply tried to emulate in my fathering. Thank you for always being there. It means so much knowing you are proud of the father I have become.

Clarence's Special Thanks: Thanks to Brenda, my wife, and my girls, Christina, Michelle, and Andrea as I'm still a work in progress. I'm so grateful to my Dad, the late Clarence F. Shuler, Sr. for the example he set for me and to Gary Chapman, Bob Cook and Don Sharp, all of whom have served as my alternate Dads.

Authors' Contact information:
Dr. Shears: jkshears@uncc.edu.
Twitter: @dadsknow
Dr. Shuler: clarencefs@gmail.com
www.clarenceshuler.com
Twitter: @clarenceshuler

What All Dads Should Know

WHAT ALL DADS SHOULD KNOW

"Mothers have the incredible privilege of birthing life; fathers have the incredible privilege of shaping that life."

Dr. Clarence Shuler

WHAT ALL DADS SHOULD KNOW
DR. JEFFREY SHEARS
DR. CLARENCE SHULER

FATHERING MATTERS

INTRODUCTION

In my life, I take on many roles that make up who I am. I am a husband, coach, professor, friend, brother, colleague, son, and a host of others, but the one that truly defines me is my role as a father. Quite simply, my very essence is that of being a dad.

The phrase, "You are what you do!" comes to mind when I recognize fathering as my primary role. Most of my daily routine is filled with fathering activities such as care giving, transporting, educating, and providing financially for my family. In addition to these activities, the majority of my thoughts and plans for the future are that of a father. How I spend and save money, where I live, where I spend my time, even how I plan my daily calendar are all filtered through the context of being a father. My role as a father shows the world to me in a different light and since becoming a father; my world has been forever changed. Everything in my life is now in the context of being a dad.

How does one get to this point? For me, transitioning into this alter ego of "Dad" happened rather late well into my thirties. It is safe to assume that before fatherhood, I must have certainly been occupied with other things. I mean, I lived for over thirty years doing something, serving some purpose, before becoming a father.

Reflecting on my pre-fatherhood days, I do remember that my life was busy and that I did have quite a bit of fun in college. (And by quite a bit of fun, that could be interpreted as way too much fun as it took me five and a half years to finish my bachelor's degree.) After completing my undergraduate degree, I tried to make up for lost time by focusing on my professional career and by completing graduate school. During this time, my life seemed to revolve around reaching some of life's major milestones and I have a résumé to prove it.

To be quite honest, it is extremely difficult for me to reconnect with who I was before fatherhood. To me, this pre-fatherhood guy existed a lifetime ago. I often think that he was not me at all, but rather a completely different person. This dude is so different and foreign to the person that I am now that I barely recognize him in my thoughts. He is a stranger.

Fatherhood became a reality for me on April 3, 1999. This was the day that I married Danni, officially making me Jordan's stepfather. Due to the brevity of my courtship with Danni, I had known Jordan for a little more than a year before marrying her mother. Even though Jordan and I had a relatively short period of time to get to know one another before I became her stepfather, she and I had a great relationship. I think this is in part due to the fact that I showed respect for her and her mother by keeping my distance until Danni and I were both certain that this would be a long-term relationship.

Prior to marrying Danni, we made a conscious decision to limit my interaction with Jordan until it was certain that we would get married. When we first began to date, I met Jordan but we rarely interacted for any length of time as Danni was cognizant of introducing her young daughter to numerous men. Here was this wonderful woman who recognized the importance of stability and security in her child's life, which of course made her even more attractive to me. In sharing this value, we both agreed to protect the consistency in Jordan's life by limiting my contact with her while her mother and I figured out where our relationship might lead. This meant that I didn't hang over at her house, Jordan did not accompany us on dates, and she never came to my house with her mom to visit.

It is important for dating adults with children to consider the possible negative effect of having numerous adults in the life of a child. Children thrive in stable environments, so introducing a young child to various dating partners is not good because they can become attached to those adults. There is a body of literature suggesting that children might have a higher incidence of anxiety when there is a constant change in their parent's relationships. This anxiety is only exacerbated when there is a break up.

I don't quite remember the time or date when Danni and I began to slide on our agreement of limiting my interaction with Jordan, but after a while—once she and I knew where our relationship was headed—all three of us were spending time together quite often. I began to make the conscious effort to include Jordan, who was five years old at the time, in our activities. I never wanted her to feel like I was taking her mom away from her, nor did I want to be perceived as a threat. By making it a point to include Jordan as much as possible in our activities, I was able to gain her confidence. Unless it was a movie or late event, I always requested that Danni bring Jordan along.

I have observed several buddies of mine who have also dated ladies with children and I've asked them about their experiences. Based on what I've gathered, my advice is this: If it is *not* a serious relationship that you have with the mother, don't form a relationship with the child. It will do more harm than good if it is a casual relationship. If it *is* serious, then you need to include the child in most everything you do. Remember, it's a package deal!

Becoming a father to Jordan has been a wonderful experience that I am so thankful for. As might be expected in step-parenting, there have been some rough times, but overall we have maintained a great relationship. This was due to my understanding and willingness to connect to Jordan on the level she needed. (Read more on understanding your role as a stepfather or father figure as it is discussed in detail in **Chapter 6**.)

Once Jordan and I established the "rules" of our relationship, everything seemed to work out. Jordan had an active biological father in her life, so I needed to assess my role as her stepfather. In figuring out that role, it is essential to meet the child where she is in regards to age, development, and the relationship that she has to her biological father.

Recognize what voids you can fill in your stepchild's life. This could include providing financial support, friendship, mentoring, and any other ways to care for that child. Given that fathers might serve a number of roles, it is critical for you to figure out where you might fit into the equation to best contribute to your stepchild's well-being. As a stepfather, children may need you to be a complete father or they may need you to fill some other areas of their life. Many times it is crucial to not abruptly disturb the normal flow of things and as stated previously, to figure out where you best fit in the big picture.

So here I am in the "big picture" with Jordan, and soon after settling into this role, I'm granted another blessing. A newborn named Jiera entered my life. I went from single guy, to stepfather and husband of a pregnant wife in less than two years. I don't waste time! Before we knew it, Danni and I were quickly immersed in the whole "we're pregnant" thing. I must admit that I never felt pregnant nor did I look pregnant, but Danni did, and it wasn't one of those easy little cute pregnancies either. Trust me, I was like, "wow!" and boy was I given a quick crash course in pregnancy education early on. With Danni's morning sickness, moodiness, and emotional outbursts, I did what I thought was right, but Danni will probably say that I was the worst husband any pregnant woman ever had. I might agree on some levels, but I could not imagine her going through the pregnancy alone. Fathers are beneficial to mothers when they are present and **Chapter 5** provides specific ideas on how fathers can help support mothers in their role.

Childbirth is an experience like no other for women of course, but also for fathers. While witnessing the birth of their child, many men are overcome with emotion, but often a sense of helplessness and fear is heightened at this time. You're left feeling like maybe you don't quite have it together and now you have this helpless child depending on you.

I felt this overwhelming responsibility of being a provider to my children, and this is a common fathering role many men identify with and is further discussed in **Chapter 2**.

When Jiera was born, I was barely making ends meet as I worked part-time and was a full-time graduate student. Needless to say, it was rough financially, but having Jiera was such a rewarding experience.

One benefit of working part-time is that it allowed me the privilege of spending much of my time at home with my infant daughter, becoming her primary caregiver. And as with most new parents, I was immersed in child development literature to read up on all the growth spurts, milestones and other developments my Jiera would soon enter. Even in her toddler years and after her little sister was born, a friend of mine joked that Jiera and I were tied at the hip. She was always with me. **Chapter 2** introduces the concept of fathering across all of the developmental stages, detailing the necessity of fathers during the formative years.

Bringing home our newborn Jiera was quite an adjustment. For starters, our two-bedroom townhouse provided fairly cramped living conditions. Jordan had her own room and Danni and I kept Jiera's crib in our room. Since Danni breast fed, there was no "need" for me to get up for nightly feedings, but I got up with her anyway. I was so connected with that little baby that as soon as she stirred at night, I would get her from her crib and bring her to our bed so Danni could feed her.

That was a great time for me as a parent. Here was this precious ball of clay that I could mold into a great little person. All of the information that I knew about early infant development literature—particularly on cognitive development—was used on Jiera. In fact, I'm pretty sure Jiera runs her mouth constantly today thanks to the focus that I placed on her cognitive development early on. That girl has never met a conversation she didn't like.

When Jiera was about two years old, I was distance teaching and the family rode along with me to Grand Junction, Colorado to spend the day while I taught my class. She was with me as I was loading up the car, and playing around, I put her car seat up front with me. I was not intending for her to sit there the whole time, but when Danni got to the car, she and my other daughters hopped in the back, allowing Jiera to ride up front with me.

The trip is over three hours, winding over 300 miles through the Rocky Mountains. On the way, the girls quickly fell asleep in the car, except for Jiera. She talked and asked questions the entire trip. She went on and on with, "Dad, what's that? Why? Daddy, did you see that? Why?" and so on. Danni woke up a few hours later and asked, "Is that baby still talking?" Jiera sat up front and talked the entire trip and hasn't stopped talking since! Today, if we want to know anything that happens at the house, at school, or in our neighborhood—and especially if we want the very detailed version—she is the one to ask!

Now, you would think that children that come from the same stock would be similar in personality, but any parent with more than one child will be quick to tell you that this assumption is false. As I previously alluded, we added to our family with the birth of Jadah in February 2002.

It is interesting how both of my biological children differ in their early developmental stages as well as in their fathering needs. One thing I have learned from my fathering experience is that fathers have to understand each child's individual personality in order to serve the various roles that their kids need.

During Danni's pregnancy with Jadah, I was better equipped for my husband role because I knew what to expect. I wasn't nearly as anxious with Jadah's birth as I had been with Jiera's and figured that I could handle whatever came along. The stress of parenting is included in the territory that comes with being a father, but I found it manageable this go-round. I had learned that my fathering responsibilities go far beyond attempting to financially provide for my children. I share how a father's interaction is beneficial to his daughters in **Chapter 3.**

Most of us recognize that fathering is not an easy job. If it were, we would certainly not have so many deadbeat dads that are uninvolved in their child's life. When describing the difficulties of fatherhood, Dr. B. Courtney McBath hits the nail on the head in the following list:

REASONS WHY FATHERHOOD IS THE MOST DIFFICULT JOB A MAN CAN EVER HAVE

- There are so many poor examples standing on every corner to influence you.

- The job *never* ends because your adult kids need fathers (and money) too.
- The pay is ridiculously low and the benefits usually take 20 years before they kick in.
- You never really know if you are doing a good job or not.
- People seldom notice or appreciate the "good" dads because the "dog" dads get all the attention.
- The kids you are trying to help often treat you like you're their enemy.
- You're molding your children into something, but often you don't exactly know what you are molding them into, so the goal is often unclear.
- How your kids turn out is such a serious reflection of you that your own pride often gets in the way of raising them.
- Only God really knows the wrestling in a man's heart when it comes to the safety, stability, and success of his kids.

As a research scientist, I love asking questions, analyzing data, comparing data from multiple sources, and coming up with credible and reliable answers. Now, I want to explore if fathering is considered easy or hard from a religious perspective. It is for this reason that **Chapter 7** of this book will view fathering from that angle.

I wanted to expand the focus of this book, so I invited my colleague, Dr. Clarence Shuler, to assist me with the writing of this book. Like me, Clarence serves multiple roles in life, but one of his most prized roles is that of father to his three daughters (all in their early twenties). His study and experience in the field of religion will help extend this book's focus. Results of his work are incorporated throughout the book. Dr. Shuler and I will refer to ourselves in the book as Jeff and Clarence because we want you to consider us your friends or even brothers in this fathering adventure. Clarence's contributions will not be cited throughout the book, but know that the bulk of his work is in **Chapter 7**, Christian Fathering, which we both think will be helpful to all fathers, regardless of their personal religious views.

My father remains an enormous influence in my life. Much of **Chapter 4** discusses the importance of fathers *being there* for their sons. You often hear that "it takes a man to raise a man" and although there are many great men who were raised by their mothers, one could argue that these men had some male role model in their lives to offer a sense of direction and positive masculine roles. Chapter 4 discusses in detail why fathers are the key to their sons' lives.

Hopefully, you'll benefit from the fathering experiences that Clarence and I share as he and I have benefitted from each other's fathering experiences.

We are certainly not perfect fathers. I'm sure that we would both do some things differently if we could go back and start over, but the reality is that we can't go back. But as you read this book, you'll discover that is it not too late for you to be the father you always wanted to be. Most of all, Clarence and I want you to know that your fathering really does matter!

DR. JEFFREY SHEARS

WHAT DADS DO

CHAPTER I

Ask just about anyone if a mother is essential to her child—especially a very young child—and you'll probably hear an emphatic "Yes" in response. That same person may tell you that a father also plays an important role, and if they do, I doubt they would be as enthusiastic about it. But father involvement can influence and transform the lives of children just the same. Unfortunately, some fathers are ignorant of this fact and their ignorance is *the* primary contributor to the lack of father involvement in America today.

For most of us dads, we realize that we have to financially provide for our children. The courts and government also agree that providing for our children is a basic or foundational aspect of fatherhood. Seldom do you hear of a judge sentencing a dad to spending time with his daughter or hugging his son. Our judicial courts' perspective is, as long as you are sending the checks, then you are serving your role as a dad. Fathering involves so much more than money! Our society needs to move beyond this limited concept that the only significant role of a father is to serve as a provider.

My father was there for me, and was an excellent role model throughout my childhood. He worked hard to provide the material things for us that he did not have growing up as a child, and in addition to that, he spent time with us. I'm not sure if he consciously knew how he positively influenced me as I grew up, but it is through his influence that I was able to realize how necessary fathers are to their children.

Most kids want to spend time with their fathers. This time doesn't necessarily have to be spent doing anything specific or extraordinary. My summers were mostly spent hanging with my dad at his auto body shop. His shop was hot, dusty, and junky, but it was great because I could hang with my dad there. As an entrepreneur, my dad worked quite a bit, so I didn't see him much during the school year; but the summers were ours. I would get up at the crack of dawn and stay with him at his shop all day.

Even as a kid, I enjoyed the responsibility that came with spending my days in Dad's shop. As his helper, I was in charge of running to the store for him, or watching the place when he went on errands. My days at work with Dad taught me how hard he worked to provide for us. Today I try to emulate his work ethic in providing for my own family.

My dad and I weren't much for words and we really didn't need them. We played ball. I helped him at his auto body shop after school and on the weekends. Yet, despite all the time we spent together, we rarely talked. We would ride around in the car for miles without saying a word to each other, but I knew I could trust and depend on him. And like most boys, I did get into trouble every now and then, and at those times, Dad disciplined me when necessary. No matter what, I knew that if I needed anything, he would bend over backwards to provide it.

Like many teens, I took most of this for granted, never fully appreciating my dad. It took an incident that happened in college to make me realize how lucky I really am to have him as my dad. My fraternity got into trouble for a prank my junior year in college, and my dismissal from school was a very real and scary possibility. Our case went to district court and then to arbitration. Community service was my court- ordered judgment. This process taught me how stupid it was to participate in such a prank as well as showing me the value of weighing the consequences of my actions.

As can be expected, my dad was livid about my predicament! Let's just say he used some choice words that won't be written here. As disgusted as he was, he stood by me through my day in court and even through the arbitration procedure. Although it was a fraternity ordeal with a number of my fraternity brothers charged, my dad was the *only* father who was there. During this scary time, I realized what a good dad I had. This ordeal forever changed my perspective of him.

THE NEED FOR FATHERS

Increasingly, research confirms that men have a critical influence in the lives of children. Much of this research is the result of social scientists' desire to understand how infants and children develop, as well as their desire to find the best child-rearing practices. Early efforts to understand how parenting attitudes and practices affect children often focused just on mothers. The prevailing thought was that mothers were the primary caregivers of children, so a few generations ago it was the norm to view the mother's role as the dominant influence. As a result, the overwhelming majority of the historical literature on child development places its focus on the necessity of mothers.

When one takes the historical aspect of these studies into consideration, it's difficult to be overly critical of these early efforts for not including fathers. Fathers generally were not participants in this research, but occasionally, some researchers would ask mothers about the father of the child. Consequently, most of the early fathering research studies were flawed because they used the mother's reports as proxies for the father's parenting attitudes and activities.

From these early studies, one might deduce from this lack of attention to fathers that dads are not a substantial factor in child rearing; however, there has recently been an increase in empirical research and governmental policy pertaining to father involvement. Even though some of this information appears negative, take for example the "deadbeat dad," much of it is positive because it provides information about fathers and their roles in the family.

Much of the research has examined the outcomes for children raised with a positive father figure in their lives. Numerous research studies found that with a positive father presence, children had increased levels of cognitive abilities, school performance, and social competence. When younger children were studied, they were found to have higher levels of socialization when their father was present. This may be partially attributed to the fact that fathers are more likely to be involved in social activities and physical play interactions, serving as a social playmate for children under the age of three. The natural tendency of fathers to participate in physical play with their child suggests parenting is different across gender lines. Studies support this by suggesting that fathering is different than mothering because fathers average more play time with their children than mothers do (Lamb and Lamb, 1976), are more playful and less restrictive than mothers (Lamb, 1997; Yogman, 1981), and praise their infants more during physical play (Clarke-Stewart, 1978).

This isn't a jab at mothers; it's just that mothers tend to focus more on the feeding, dressing, and nurturing side of parenting. After their nurturing and basic care duties, moms often feel that play isn't a priority, or sometimes they are just too tired to do so. Thus, there is a benefit of having a male spouse to step in as a teammate to help with parenting from a more playful perspective.

Additionally, some researchers may argue that the level of involvement and engagement with your child is strongly correlated to residential status. Even with mixed results on this population, numerous studies have found fathers not residing in the same home with their child were still actively involved in their child's daily life, particularly when it was supported by the mother. Data from the longitudinal study, "Utrecht Study of Adolescent Development" (Spruijt et al., 2001) was examined to determine whether different family structures, including intact, divorced, and widowed families, influenced the well-being of adolescents and young adults (Spruijt et al., 2001). The findings indicated that the adolescents of intact families with a healthy relationship have the best physical and psychological well-being compared to single woman-headed families, with the latter group more likely to engage in early sexual activity, smoking, alcohol consumption and drug use. However, individuals who came from a widowed family scored only slightly less than individuals from intact healthy families. This suggests that the death of a parent is usually associated with positive memories and a more positive adaptation compared to parental divorce.

INVOLVED FATHERS

More literature has examined the non-residential father, attempting to measure if these fathers are as actively involved as residential fathers. This research literature is inconsistent in that although these fathers may be actively involved, they are not as involved as residential fathers. Research results get murky as non-residential fathers may have a desire to be as involved as residential fathers, but have other difficulties, such as limited custody, court orders, restraining orders, problems with mother, etc., preventing them from doing so.

Attempting to learn more about the roles fathers play in the lives of children, research has also examined the level of interaction fathers have with their children. These studies reveal that fathers are actively involved in the lives of their children. Additionally, reports taken by mothers concerning the activities of fathers support that fathers are active with their children. Studies of fathers and their engagement with their child consistently offer that fathers are involved on numerous levels.

ROLES—MR. MOM?

So much of what was known about fathers just fifty years ago has changed dramatically. Much of this is due to historical research on fathers who were from middle class Anglo samples, or from studies of mothers' reports on the dad's activities and attitudes. Parenting in general has also changed during the last fifty years and is moving to a more authoritative parenting style. A lot of what we know about fathering is derived from the fact that there is an emphasis on studying fathering in the context of race, culture, and income levels, as all these things influence fathering attitudes and practices. For example, many low income African-American fathers report participating in more care giving activities than other dads. This is especially interesting given the fact that many of these care giving activities were considered mothering roles fifty years ago. Anglo dads reported participating in more cognitive activities with their infants than other dads. Plus, income tends to have an effect on fathering attitudes as lower income dads tend to be more authoritative in their parenting styles than higher income men.

Other factors which have impacted fathering are the divorce rate, resulting in an increase in blended families, and more mothers in the work force. These factors must be considered in the fathering issue because they have changed family dynamics. Families today are vastly different from the families our grandparents were raised in during the 1950's - 1970's. Despite these major changes in the American family, our roles as fathers remain crucial to the success of our children.

What roles men serve as dads is not always understood, even by most men. Due to human nature, we are often confined to our experiences with our father, or the representations of fathers we see on TV or in our communities. One study of inner city teen parents attempted to gauge the level of fathering by asking both parents about the baby's father. In many instances, both the mother and father expressed that the dad was an excellent parent. When asked why highly rated dads were good, both parents talked about how he came by once or twice a month or bought the baby some diapers or shoes.

Fathering has to be taken in the context of what one might consider good fathering. Coming by to visit a couple times a month isn't good fathering. This suggests that an aspect of the fathering issue is not being aware of our irreplaceable value and that how we play our roles tremendously affects our children's lives! So we need a fundamental understanding of the crucial impact of the influence that men have on their children, an understanding of how to be an effective father, and specifically what roles a father might play as the primary male figure in his child's life.

Researchers like Pleck and Palcovtz have theorized what it means to be a father and the roles men play. Understanding that children model behavior is a key toward successful fathering, which means we have to be on our best behavior at all times. We need to model behaviors which will impress upon our children the values we want them to emulate. Our goal is consistency, not perfection, nor hypocrisy, and we must be careful not to send our children mixed messages.

CHANGES IN ROLES

Over the past few generations, the roles of fathers have changed. Traditional research on fathers suggests that society's definition of fathering and the role of a father is ever evolving. Fulfilling the role of a good father, as expected in colonial times, probably will not suffice in the modern era. Understanding the expectations that mothers have of fathers is crucial. One perspective on the fathering role is that we are fathers because of the children we raise; without children there would be no fathers. In other words, our children help to dictate what our roles are in their lives.

In colonial America, a father's primary responsibilities were that of provider and moral teacher or guide for his children. This role changed as our country moved to the industrial age with the "breadwinner" becoming the dominant role of fathers, placing less emphasis on the responsibility of moral teacher or guide. During the 1930's through the 1940's, the "sex-role model" became the dominant model of good fathering.

Much of our view of fathering is centered on being a provider for the child, which was an early foundational criterion of the fathering role. Fathers have been viewed as a resource provider for the necessities of their children. The fathering literature clearly demonstrates that as fathers serve this essential role, their children benefit according to quality of life indicators. However, men must not limit themselves to the notion that good fathering is only being a supporter and provider,

Expectations of fathers have expanded due to major changes in the dynamics of the American family over the last forty years. Although the significance of providing for one's child should not be minimized, if we minimize or limit good fathering to only that of a provider, we would miss the positive effects that a father's presence has on children. Consequently, social science is being forced to understand more about how the fathering role is adapting to the demands of the modern family.

Currently, the nurturing father (Lamb, 2000) fills an appropriate fathering role. As today's mothers also work outside the home to become breadwinners, this modern father is at the request of his children to be more nurturing. Throughout the transition of fathering roles, many were still trying to fulfill the earlier role that focused on the providing aspect of fathering, only to have the role shift towards nurturing. With this transition, today's father may be required to serve multiple roles such as moral teacher, breadwinner, role model, and nurturer. To put it plainly, as soon as you think you have the present fathering roles mastered, your child, your child's mother, or society, it seems, suggests—or blatantly commands—that you add another dimension to fathering.

Today's father most commonly highlights his role of provider, disciplinarian, protector, entertainer, socializer, teacher, source of affection, support for mother, and caregiver when he considers how he serves his family. Often, I separate these roles into traditional and contemporary roles. The traditional roles include provider, disciplinarian, protector, entertainer, socializer, and teacher. The more contemporary roles place the father as a source of affection, support for mother, and caregiver. We have already established that most fathers understand the necessity of their role of provider. Sometimes, we may be in a situation in which we cannot provide for all of our family's needs due to job loss, incarceration, etc., but I believe that we as fathers should always at least attempt to get our children what they need.

DISCIPLINARIAN

Disciplinarian is another traditional role that fathers recognize, and the importance of this role should not be minimized. All kids need discipline. Clint Howard, the child star of the TV show, *Gentle Ben* and his brother, the now famous movie director Ron Howard, who played the role of a little boy named Opie on the *Andy Griffith Show* and later, a teenager in *Happy Days*, tells how they were both spoiled by the adult actors that they worked with. He says that in order to keep them in line, their dad would thump them upside their heads whenever they got full of themselves. Clint said that they needed that discipline and it made them feel loved!

My own dad knew the role of disciplinarian very well and he made sure he served that role to the fullest. He would probably say that I got away with more than I should have, but I don't remember it that way. "Wait 'till your dad gets home!" or "I'm going to tell your dad!" were common threats that my mom used on my brother and I. It's funny though, because these same threats don't really work with my kids. I confess, my girls probably would giggle if my wife threatened them with "Wait 'til your daddy gets home." But I do consider myself a disciplinarian of sorts. I am a relatively patient guy and that probably was more of an issue for my dad in his interactions with my brother. It didn't really matter as much with me. Keep in perspective that my dad was raising boys and I have a house full of girls. So I rarely come home to discover something is broken or torn, and my girls seem to be much better behaved than my brother and I were as kids. But they do recognize that I can get fairly perturbed and will lay down the law when it comes to school, grades and homework. I don't play around regarding those issues.

In 5th grade, we lived in a second floor apartment with a balcony. And like a lot of kids in my neighborhood, I was a latch key kid a few days a week because my mother was in school. I had a key to our apartment, but no matter how much I tried, I could never remember that stupid key. I tried tying it on a string and putting it around my neck, safety pinning it in my backpack, or putting it in my sneakers. More often than not, I would leave the darn thing at home. When that happened, I would have to wait around somewhere until my mom got home almost two hours later.

As an adventure-seeking fifth-grade boy, it didn't take too many lock-out incidents before I conceived a way to climb up the wall and pull myself up on the balcony to get into the house. Soon after coming up with this new way to get into the house, I started to "accidentally" leave my key at home more often. Well, Dad figured out what I was doing and stated as a matter of fact, "Don't climb the balcony again because you could fall and get hurt and there might not be anyone around to help you if this happens." Being the obedient son that I was, I began taking my key with me again, but that was short-lived.

After two weeks of faithfully carrying my key, I came home from school one day to discover that I had left it in my room again. The balcony looked so inviting because I knew the sliding door perched up there was unlocked, granting me entry into my home. I knew that I could easily stand and pull myself up just like I had so many times before. So I did it, but this time as I triumphantly threw my legs over the balcony rails, I could see my dad sitting on the sofa watching me. Given this scenario, I began to climb back down, but my dad told me that I might as well come in through the balcony, seeing that I was already up.

So here I am, with this deer in the headlights look on my face, and here is my dad basically unmoving. And without saying much else, he grabbed his coat and went back to work. He didn't need to say anything because silence truly speaks volumes, especially when you're caught red-handed! I knew what was coming to me and I knew I'd have to wait a little while for it. Dad always disciplined us before our bedtime, giving me the afternoon and evening to dwell on the incident.

Our bedtime was at nine o'clock every night, unless we took a nap that day so we could stay up to watch Monday Night Football. My night time routine involved doing homework, eating dinner with Mom, and playing with my brother before going to bed. On this particular evening, I thought that if I could make it to bedtime, I would be safe because that meant dad forgot about our little balcony incident. Sure enough, and to my relief, nine o'clock came and off to bed I went. I was saved by my dad working late that night!

After lying in the bed for a short while, I heard my dad come in from a long day of work. He had left the house before I got up for school and was just coming in after nine o'clock at night. I knew he was probably exhausted and thought surely he had other things on his mind than spanking my behind, so I settled back in to get some rest. I tried as hard as I could to fall asleep at that moment. As I was desperately attempting to fall asleep, my bedroom light suddenly came on and Dad walked in. He said, "About you climbing up the balcony today."

My dad had an evil way of disciplining us. Of course it was nothing abusive because he never spanked us while he was angry, but he definitely got his point across! He would talk with us for what seemed an eternity about why we were getting spanked. He wanted to make sure we knew and understood the repercussions of our actions. I wondered later if he would have gone through with the spanking if we questioned why he was spanking us. My mother has joked that my dad's pre-spanking talks lasted so long that she would forget that he was supposed to just give us a spanking. As I got older, I would think, "Give me my licks so I don't have to hear this sermon." In retrospect, I am appreciative of my dad's concern and that he never hit us in anger.

LIKE CEDRIC-THE ENTERTAINER: WHO ME?

We may not be as funny as professional comedians, but one role that seems to come naturally to fathers is that of entertainer. This is a playmate role. Much of the literature surrounding the study of this role discusses that men naturally gravitate into the playmate role with their children, particularly once they become old enough to rough house with. When my girls were really little, I loved to do little nursery songs like *Patty Cake* and *Itsy Bitsy Spider* with them, but the real fun began when they got a little older.

When they started toddling about, I could spin them and toss them up in the air and this is when my fathering instinct really kicked in. There is some research literature suggesting that this interaction between father and child is a prerequisite for self regulation, which is the ability to regulate one's emotions. Children who have fathers who are actively involved in their lives tend to have a higher level of self regulation than children who don't. Perhaps this is why fathers are instinctively wired to serve the entertainer role.

TEACHER

Teaching is a key role and usually comes naturally to fathers. Teaching encompasses being both a role model in addition to teaching life skills to children. One way I fulfill this teaching role in my home is by helping the girls with their homework. Over the summer, when there is no assigned homework, we spend a lot of time staying abreast with our math skills. In that sense, I am comfortable serving my teacher role.

When one considers the many life skills that fathers teach to their children, driving may very well be one of the most prominent. We're currently experiencing the teaching of this life skill in my family. Jordan just got her driving permit. She has always been curious about driving a car with a manual transmission. Well, seeing that this is a job that I am naturally hardwired to do, I took on the task of teaching her. Jordan and I spent several Sundays driving around a large empty parking lot in my stick shift car for those lessons on dumping clutches and easing into gear.

Given my natural inclination as a father to serve this teaching role, I am always trying to teach, even when I think it may be falling on deaf ears. Let's take the "Boy Talk" for example. Jordan does not want to discuss boys with me, which is understandable. It's an awkward talk for both of us. Probably most girls would prefer to skip having this talk with their dad. But this is a necessary and critical talk to have. It's better that she learns some lessons about boys from me rather than from her silly girlfriends and *definitely not* from the boys that want to date her.

CAREGIVER & NURTURER

As fathering has changed over time, it has expanded to the more contemporary role of serving as a source of affection, support of mother, and caregiver. This paradigm shift in the fathering can partly be explained by the aforementioned, such as mothers in the workplace and co-parenting families. So men have adapted to what our children, mothers and families need from us and men are embracing these responsibilities. Serving in these roles is both fun and rewarding. Most fathers serve them admirably. The joy that I receive when a daughter runs into my arms after school, yelling *"Daddy!"* is one such reward and I welcome that moment every day. It is imperative for us to figure out what we do as fathers and then help to educate other men by modeling these behaviors. We may not normally serve in this capacity, but we can learn to do so. Our children and our grandchildren are the benefactors of us functioning in these roles as our present families will influence our future families for generations to come.

PRIMARY INFLUENCER

My friend Clarence always begins his Dads Seminar with the following statement, "NO ONE WILL HAVE A GREATER IMPACT ON MY CHILDREN EITHER POSITIVELY OR NEGATIVELY THAN ME!" His first statement is followed by a second statement: "YES, THERE IS PEER PRESSURE, BUT IT PALES IN COMPARISON TO YOU!"

As stated earlier, there is a huge investment on our part that takes many years for us to see the end product of our years of toil and sweat. But rest assured that the research literature identifies some specific benefits to children with active dads. A majority of this empirical literature has focused on father involvement, father-infant emotional relationships, and father-child activities. Examining these areas has resulted in a number of conclusions regarding the impact of fathers throughout the various developmental stages of childhood. This research suggests that fathers are crucial in their children's lives. There are positive effects when fathers are involved in the lives of their children in addition to financial support. The next chapter discusses some of these fathering roles in the context of developmental stages and offers some of the benefits of fathering.

Some roles may be difficult for non-residential fathers. Research literature is consistent in that although non-residential fathers may be actively involved, they are not as involved as residential fathers. Much of the literature suggests that co-parenting can be difficult for some parents with a non-residential father. As difficult as it may be, parents have to co-exist for the sake of the children after they have severed their relationship.

Parents may need to seek professional mediation or other help to assist them in transitioning from a romantic to a co-parenting status. It is worth the cost and effort for both the parents and for the children involved. In order to make a co-parenting relationship work, fathers need to overlook their dislike for the mother and instead focus on the love for their child and the strong need to be involved in his or her life. Although some scholars would argue that the level of involvement and engagement with the child is strongly correlated to residential status, studies have found that non-residential fathers are actively involved in their child's daily life, particularly when it is supported by the child's mother.

As we understand our roles in our children's lives, we can become better fathers as we cease to be passive and begin fathering with a purpose. In fathering with a purpose, we need to examine the various fathering roles in detail.

CLARENCE'S CORNER

Jeff and I must be related because our fathers are so much alike. Like Jeff, my late father seemed to always work two or three jobs and he is still my hero. One of his jobs involved working as a janitor for thirty-eight years for R.J. Reynolds Tobacco Company. He worked hard and he was very smart, even though his formal education was limited to the eighth grade. My sister, Jean, inherited most of his smart genes. Even though he was an extremely quiet and serious man, he had his funny side. Without question, he was fun to be around and I just wanted to hang out with him no matter what he was doing.

With all of his years working on my grandfather's South Carolina farm, and all the other physical labor that he did, my dad developed an incredible physique. Unfortunately, I didn't inherit that either. I thought he was Superman, but stopping for gas on a trip to South Carolina in 1964 re-enforced my perspective when three white men began calling him all kinds of derogatory names.

You see, my sister and I grew up during a time of racial unrest in the mid 1950's and 60's and Dad received quite a bit of verbal abuse, yet he and many other African American men of that era had a quiet dignity. My dad told my mom, Jean, and me to stay in the car. I asked my mother, "Mom, why is Daddy letting those men talk to him like that?!" I'm ashamed to say, I momentarily thought my dad wasn't being brave. Mom replied, "Baby, he is being as brave as he knows how to be. If he responds to those men or even looks at them, there's no telling what they would do to him. But your dad is more concerned what they would do to us." That day, Dad was protecting us even if it might cost him his life and from that point on, he became my hero for life, despite any disagreements we had or ever would have. Like Jeff and his father, Dad and I didn't talk much, but unlike Jeff and his dad, we often had conflict. Also, unlike Jeff, I didn't develop much of a work ethic. My dad worked hard and I was lazy, so naturally, we clashed!

Growing up, my god was basketball—I blame that on being born in North Carolina—so I was always playing ball while my dad was always working. In retrospect, I wish I had used the opportunities that I was given to learn things from him, like how to work on a car, repair things around the house, etc.; not just to be handy, but to have learned more about him and have more time with him. I often told my dad I would earn a basketball scholarship and his facial expression reflected his thoughts on that being a long shot, but he never discouraged me nor did he crush my dream. I was happy to put his pessimism to rest as I did earn that basketball scholarship and was even given the opportunity to play against national and Olympic basketball teams. I believe that my basketball accomplishments were a result of my dad refraining from discouraging me away from my dream. One of the greatest gifts he gave me was that he never told me that there was anything that I couldn't do.

Dad created a safe, loving environment in our home by the way he loved and freely expressed his love for my mother. He also loved us kids. My sister was definitely a "Daddy's girl." When I was small, my dad hugged and kissed me (not on the lips). I think in his wisdom, he was trying to break the cycle of non-touching men in the Shuler family. As a six or seven-year-old, I asked him to stop kissing and hugging me because I wanted to be a man. In retrospect, I wish he would have overridden my ignorant request.

Dad loved to laugh, tell jokes, and have fun. And there were those times he had to discipline me. Dad only spanked me three times in my life, but each time I thought I was going to die! Despite the terror of those spankings, I'm sure they saved my life because they kept me from taking certain risks.

My dad had an important job of being my father, through his example, discipline, and the affection that he showed, he served it well. He had many jobs to support our family and his work ethic showed me that for fathers, no matter what your job is—whether garbage collector or president of a company—don't be ashamed of it because your children aren't ashamed of you, unless you give them a reason to be. He gave us something that no one else could give and that was himself. For any father, that's the one gift they must share with their kids.

What Do You Think?

(Questions to answer for yourself, with your father if possible, in a small group, or with girlfriend or spouse)

- If your father was around, what are your boyhood memories of him?
- What about your dad's fathering do you want to emulate and why?
- What is it about your dad's fathering that you do not want to repeat with your children and why?
- How is your fathering role different from that of your dad?
- For you, what are key things you want to teach your children or what do you want your children to be?
- Would your children say you are a caregiver and/or nurturer? Why or why not?
- How do you feel about being the most influential person to your children?
- Do your children consider you an entertainer; do you make them laugh? Why or why not?
- If asked, what kind of father would your children say you are?
- What memories do you want your children to have of you? Why?

FATHERING ACROSS DEVELOPMENTAL STAGES

CHAPTER 2

Age-appropriate responses and interactions with our children are essential in our fathering. For example, your ten-year-old son may not want to play patty cake, nor will your six-month-old be able to play a pickup game of basketball. Fathering roles will span across each developmental stage of your children. Exactly how you father will be dictated by the developmental level or age of your child. Earlier, I commented that fathers are flexible and hard-wired to meet their children's changing needs. Although there is no perfect model of fathering, there are numerous activities that fathers can do that are essential for their child's positive development. Parenting issues which are critical in fathering our children from infancy to adolescence will be explored in this chapter.

Infants

Men are influential in the lives of infants and this is highlighted by the considerable amount of literature on early infant development that describes a father's influence on his child. Much of my own interest and research has examined the roles that fathers play throughout infancy and early childhood. My particular interest is in understanding the value of the interaction between young children and their fathers. Society's low expectations of fathers at this stage of development intrigues me, so my interest is twofold: (1) *How do fathers connect with newborns?* and (2) *How does this interaction strengthen the child-father bond long term?*

Historical research suggests that men traditionally have not been exactly sure of their fathering role with a newborn. Men have played a supporting role by helping the mother both financially and for the occasional diaper change, but for the most part, men have not been made aware of the life-changing impact that they have on their infants. Sometimes, fathers just don't get the credit they deserve when it comes to caring for an infant. Much of the popular media would have us believe that fathers are all thumbs in their interactions with their newborns, while mothers tend to be particularly protective and may possibly monopolize the time with the child. Let's face it, many women believe that the care of a small child is "women's work" and they may have issues with fathers having too much responsibility with their baby. Some women may even become jealous of the father when he assumes more of an active role of caring for the child.

FATHER BONDING

Men and women alike should understand that a fathers' interaction with his new child is very important. During this stage, children learn who daddy is. More significantly, it is a crucial time when fathers bond with or become attached to their child, which would seem to lower the father's chances of becoming an absentee dad. Research suggests that it is this early attachment with the child that promotes fathering during the life course. More recent research revealed that men, just as women, have hormonal changes at the birth of their child. According to research, these hormonal changes allow fathers to experience a greater level of attachment with his newborn. This is demonstrated by literature suggesting that incarcerated fathers, or those who are physically separated from their newborn, have a more difficult time bonding with their child; which leads to the conclusion that men's presence in their infant's life is a critical time between father and child.

As a result of this physiological phenomenon, I encourage new fathers to focus on being an integral part of their newborn's life. Such involvement may include rescuing your child whenever she first awakes for a feeding or diaper change. By doing this, your child will learn to associate you as a protector and nurturer, because when she cries, you are there to rescue and comfort her. For example, when Jiera would wake up at night for her feeding, I would be the one to get up, in a sense "rescuing" her, even though my wife was breast feeding. Certainly, there was no need for both of us to get up at three o'clock in the morning and lose precious sleep, but I understood how significant it was for my daughter to depend on me as part of this process. As a result of my actions, she learned at a very early age to become dependent not only on her mother, but her daddy too! This *team parenting* was also a benefit to my wife, specifically in knowing that she wasn't parenting alone.

Alone time with daddy is another indispensable element in a young child's development as it provides security. I'm not telling Mom to go to Tahiti for two weeks. She can still be in the home. But you, the father, need to be totally attentive to your child for a few hours without the interaction of anybody else, including mom. Both Jiera and Jadah spent considerable time as infants lying on my chest while I was on the sofa, watching TV or reading. When Jiera was an infant, I was a graduate student so she was with me quite a bit. She was involved in all of my daily activities, whether it was shopping, cleaning, or studying. I talked through my activities with her as well. Whatever I was reading, whether it was my dissertation, the ESPN sports page, or a list of cooking ingredients, if she was with me, I would read it to her. I did this for Jadah as well. This was a conscious decision I made so I could bond with my daughters. This "quantity" time spent with my girls early on later turned into "quality" time. It helped strengthen the bond between us, and by spending moments with your child doing everyday activities, you can also develop a a strong bond.

Generally, a man's voice and interaction with a newborn is very different than a woman's. It has been my observation that babies gravitate more to interaction with a man. Recently, I experienced this when my family was interacting with a single mother's infant son. My three daughters were all over him, but once I entered the room, this baby boy became fixated on me. And once I picked him up, he only wanted to be held by me. I believe a man's involvement with his baby is a necessity because children need to interact with both their mothers and fathers.

Fathers need to be students of their children, paying close attention in order to learn their child's unique needs and wants. A better way of saying this is that dads need to train the child according to his or her natural inclinations. If the child has some artistic talent, nurture that area. And as children age, encourage them to pursue their interest, but it must be *for* your child, not for you to live vicariously through him or her.

TODDLERS

As a new dad, each day upon arriving home, a priority for me would be to hold and get a whiff of my babies' smell. I just loved breathing in the smell of my clean babies; notice I used the word clean; not all baby smells are easy to inhale. Although I looked forward to coming home to them as infants, the real fun started when they became toddlers. They didn't seem so fragile and their ability to have more interaction was exciting. Every day was new and adventurous, mostly because of my expectation that they would reach some new developmental milestone or demonstrate an increase in potential. The anticipation of these new developments kept (and still keeps) fatherhood exciting.

Most fathers are more comfortable with their children when they reach toddler age because of the usual increase in the child's level of interaction with dad, so I'm not alone in my feelings, and research actually supports this fact. This toddler age is a transition point in which fathers typically take over their natural role as playmate. Numerous studies suggest that at this age, men spend much of their time socializing with their children as a playmate. This playmate role is probably the most frequent interactive activity that fathers provide and this is one area where fathering vastly differs from mothering.

As playmates, fathers are much more likely to play with their child in rough and tumble ways and this type of play has some unique benefits to children. One in particular is that children who have active fathers have increased levels of self regulation than children who have absent fathers. As you might imagine, a father comes home from work and his young child is playing quietly on the floor. During this quiet play time the child's activity level is fairly low or flat lined. Dad comes in, grabs the child, begins the rough and tumble play and suddenly the child's activity level is dramatically increased. Then, father sits the child back down and continues his other activities. Here the child has gone from a minimal level of activity, to a heightened level, back to a minimal level all within a few minutes. These children are able to self regulate their emotions because of their interactions with their dad.

Additionally, it is critical for a father to interact with his child because he is much more likely to allow the child to be out of his view than a mother would. I am not implying that fathers are likely to leave their child unattended in dangerous situations, but simply that fathers are much more comfortable with their child being out of their view in a secure environment. Studies have revealed that mothers become uncomfortable if their infant is out of view.

With my girls, I used the *barricade* method of supervision. I baby-proofed the house and made sure all the doors were closed to the bathroom and bedrooms. The other dangers, such as the steps, were also barricaded. Once this was accomplished, my active infant could crawl on the floor to her heart's content. This barricade method provided a safe area in which my girls could play, allowing for short periods of time that they could navigate and explore with limited supervision. Even this minor difference in parenting attitudes between mothers and fathers has been suggested to have significant benefits, as children who are allowed to explore have more developed levels of cognitive ability than children who are impeded from such activity.

For me as a father, this toddler stage provided many fun and exciting times. But I do remember how it turned simple daily activities, such as shopping, going to dinner at a restaurant, or paying a bill into major productions. Jiera and Jadah were close in age, so I had double duty in getting them dressed, packing a diaper bag, and putting them in their car seats. Thankfully, Jordan was such a great helper with her sisters, making it easier to get them ready, but it was still exhausting and time consuming to do anything outside the house with them. Once they were potty trained and diaper bags were no longer needed, "Oh Happy Day!" It was so liberating to say, "Hey girls, go get in the car." They would grab their coats, run to the car and climb into their seats. All I had to do was just buckle them in and we were off!

CHILDHOOD

Another significant milestone for children comes when they enter school. For me, that represented no more childcare fees! But more notably, it represented that my children were becoming older and finally growing out of their baby stage. Attending school all day, riding the school bus, and participating in extracurricular activities helps children become more independent and responsible. As children move to more independence, your role doesn't diminish; in some instances it becomes more of a necessity.

Think about it. Your child now spends most of his time away from the secure environment at home, while you may now spend considerable time ensuring that this new environment is a safe and nurturing place. Also, your children have to know that you are still there for them and that you're still involved, which is what most children want from their parents to help them feel secure. Such security continues to help them develop positively, emotionally, intellectually, physically, and spiritually.

For my girls, I try to stay involved in their school and after school activities. You'll find me at field days, sometimes in the cafeteria with them at lunch, and at after-school events to show them my consistent support for them. Additionally, with their homework and projects, I attempt to make sure they are having the best experience possible. Bob Stoops, Head football Coach of the University of Oklahoma Sooners, said four or five years ago during an ESPN interview that he walks his daughter to the school bus every day, then he drives his then six-year-old twin boys to school. I believe he said, "Driving them to school is the highlight of my day. We get into some amazing conversations. Football records are nice, but in the end it is your family and the Lord are really all that matter!"

My wife and I sent Jadah to a Montessori preschool for a half-day partly to prepare her for entering kindergarten later. Even then, she attended sparingly—she was truly the baby—and with the exception of those few hours a day, a few days a week, she was with either one of her parents or with her sisters. So she was always in familiar surroundings and was always viewed as the *baby*, unlike Jiera who always seemed like she was ready to go to school (she told us to leave when we took her to childcare the first day and did not shed a tear). Jadah, on the other hand, loved being at home with her familiar surroundings. When visiting friends or out somewhere, she would often comment that she was ready to go home; she was not the kid who would happily leave home. Most often, if given the choice between staying home or going somewhere with Danni or me, she would choose to stay home.

With Jadah's inclination to stay home rather than go out, I was unsure how she would handle her first day of school, but with a certain level of anxiety, I was proud my baby was going to the big school. And like any other proud daddy, I videotaped her going to school the first day, following her all the way to her classroom. It was not a good feeling for me to take her to school because I didn't think she was ready, but one thing that saved us was that big sister Jiera's second grade classroom was across the hall, so Jiera could walk Jadah to and from class daily. I'm proud to say that like most children, she was resilient, adapted, and she had a fabulous school year.

Research shows that fathering is foundational to the childhood stage. It is during this childhood stage that children become much more aware of life, values, and morals. Your interaction with your kids helps to determine who they will become. Traditional roles of provider and protector become quite apparent to your child during this period of development. Your child begins to understand that daddy is here to protect her from harm and danger. Having a house full of girls who are afraid of almost every bug they see, I am the protector from creepy crawly things and seem to be on-call constantly. Also, my children understand that I work—which is what dads are supposed to do—so we can buy things they need and want. Even the role of disciplinarian is understood when Jadah, the youngest, chastises her older sisters by saying, "You are going to get in trouble when I tell daddy!"

I enjoy being their playmate and socializing with them. At this stage, my children expect me to play with them and to be able to accompany me on errands. In my mind, all of these activities are fundamental to our relationship and thus their well-being.

TREAT THE MOTHER OF YOUR CHILD WELL

Serving as partner with their mother is one of my most crucial roles. How I treat and interact with their mother sends such a powerful message to my girls. This is so critical because it influences what kind of boy they will date, as well as the kind of man they will eventually marry. Many men understand their significance in the lives of their sons as we often suggest that it takes a man to raise a man. Such statements, although true, may minimize the effect we have on our daughters. The research literature suggests that even though we have a strong, profound direct effect on our daughters, we also have an incredible indirect effect on them through our verbal and non-verbal communication with their mothers.

Your relationship with your child's mother is a tremendously pivotal factor in blended families and co-parenting relationships. Even when the romantic relationship between parents ceases to exist, their interaction and the child's perception of their relationship should remain positive. Simply stated, our children should not be exposed to drama and negative interactions between parents. For the child's best interest, in most instances, a child is more emotionally stable if the parents are perceived to be united. This is especially true once the child becomes a teenager.

ADOLESCENCE

We've all heard of how dreadful the teen years can be for parents. It seems that the home training you thought you've instilled in your child suddenly disappears when he or she becomes a teenager. Even worse than that, your previously delightful child seems to have been replaced by a person you are not sure you even know! This is a natural progression as your influence begins to be replaced by your child's peers. Suddenly, their 15-year-old peer group has much more understanding of life than you. Even through this sometimes rocky time, your role is to continue to be the consistent presence in your teenager's life. Believe it or not, they still long for consistency and need your consistent presence and voice. According to both secular and religious youth workers, no one has a greater influence on children than their fathers. These youth workers also say that if fathers did their jobs, gangs would cease to exist or have little influence. Without parental boundaries, especially provided by fathers, teenagers often feel unloved. They will never tell you this, but all children feel secure and loved when parents say, "No," because it voices concern and shows that their parents love them. The key is consistency, not perfection.

My teenager seems to have a Dr. Jekyll and Mr. Hyde personality and you just don't know what you are going to get from day to day. Some days, she is like her old self, playful and wants to hang around you. Then the next day, she is totally different and tucks herself away in her room. But my job as a dad is to remain consistent in my interaction with her, not allowing her mood swings to dictate how I parent. My expectations of her don't change because she wants to have a bad day. No matter what mood she is in, she is still expected to complete her assigned chores and to effectively communicate politely with the entire family or she will have to pay the consequences. With these basic parenting principles in practice, I don't expect to be liked all the time, nor am I trying to be her friend. Some parents fall into the trap of wanting to be a friend to their teen and to be liked by them. My saying "No" to my girls when they want to go and hang out with certain people will benefit them later. As I explained to Jordan, "I am here for the long haul. You may or may not know your current best friend in the next ten years, so what her parents allow her to do, or where she can go, or what time she can come in does not mean much to me." Parenting teens will be discussed in more detail later.

A balancing act with teenagers is required primarily because they are in a very emotional, intellectual, physical, and spiritual transitional stage. You want them to know that you trust them, but also that you are not gullible; you too were a teenager once. Typically, trust should be earned. A parent might say, "Sure, you can go to the movies with your friends, but don't be surprised if I show up at the movie," or, "Sure, you can go hang out at your friend's house on Saturday, but don't be surprised if I call your friend's parents."

Jordan understands that I go to great lengths to verify her whereabouts because I love her. Even with my verification, there is no guarantee that she won't end up some place that I'm unaware of. We fathers all remember what it was like being a teenager! Although she is a good kid, it is only human nature for her to try to get away with something. But at least she knows that she is being monitored not to keep her from having fun, but for her safety. I am often appalled by some of the parents of Jordan's friends who allow their teens to come over for a few hours, or even to spend the night, no questions asked, without even giving so much as a phone call to verify the whereabouts of their teens and to make sure that everything checks out. Now, I may sound paranoid, but safety first, versus being sorry, resonates with me. Jordan's friends could be anywhere and parents that aren't verifying their teen's whereabouts are quite possibly allowing them to enter situations that might land them in all sorts of trouble and danger.

My goal in raising my adolescents is getting them to the maturity level where they can make consistent intelligent decisions. Consistent intelligent decisions require understanding of the possible consequences of one's actions or seeing the "big picture." No matter what may happen or what decision they make, if I question them about understanding the consequences of their actions, and if they understand the consequences and still choose to participate in whatever activity, I've done my job as a father.

As a father, if my girls say, "Daddy, I didn't know," or "You didn't tell me!" then I've failed. But even when our teens fail or make bad decisions, we still need to be parents to them. Now, much to our chagrin as parents, many of their bad teenage decisions can become much more public and detrimental in today's media-hungry society. But just like we loved them when they broke something as toddlers, we need to continue verbally communicating our love and support to them. Our love and support helps teens to deal with difficult issues in their lives as it helps them learn how to make better life choices and take responsibility for the mistakes they have made. This becomes a great life skill that can be used as they enter adulthood, which they can share with their children. So as you invest in your children, you are actually investing in your grandchildren; thus, your legacy.

ADULTS

Empirical research examining the transition of parent - child relationships as children become adults is scarce. Being cynical, we will probably first have to wait until research scientists figure out what the relationship is between mothers and adult children. Why? It is because all of the research studies have examined mom and child first, then subsequently examined dads. Sorry dads, but we're merely an afterthought! The few studies that do exist agree that as you become the father of an adult child, it is still necessary to continue serving the fathering role. Even though your relationship with your adult child will be vastly different than when he or she was younger, your presence, along with your verbal and non-verbal life examples, provide your adult child a sense of stability, security, and an effective adult model. For example, a study by Marsiglio, Hutchinson, and Cohan (2000) found that men reported looking to their own fathers as role models. Also, understanding that fathering is different than mothering, men tend to parent much more like their fathers than their mothers.

So if you are thinking that your fathering ends when your child turns 18 or 21, you are sadly mistaken! It is a lifetime commitment! Even though you may turn Junior's room into the man's room, complete with a big screen, surround sound, and leather recliner, your role as father continues. However, your responsibilities as father should change, paralleling your child's growth into adulthood. At some stage, you may have a hand in helping your adult child to mature, and helping your child as an adult can be quite a transition.

Reflecting on how the relationship I had with my father transitioned to adulthood, I realized we became closer as I got older. We became closer by spending more time together and although I was only 20 years old, my father felt that I had matured enough that he could interact with me on an equal level. He would never shy away from offering advice, but rarely bothered or followed up to make sure I had followed his advice. He gave me the freedom to accept or reject his advice, which didn't translate into a rejection of him if I didn't take it. Another major reason we became closer was because I began to confide and trust in him. I recognized what he had accomplished in his life and was really proud to have him as my dad.

He was the oldest of 12 children in the rural segregated South and he had a learning disability. Given those factors, he really did not have much of a chance in life. Yet, he provided a good life for my brother and me. As I got older, I realized how far my dad had come. No, we didn't live in luxury. He didn't own his first home until I was in the seventh grade. As a child, I remember having to be quiet, not answering the door when someone from the sheriff's office visited to talk to my dad about a bad check he had written to buy groceries for our family. We were certainly not well-off but he *stayed* with us, worked hard, and never gave up on us. Because of his hard work, my brother and I had opportunities that he was never afforded.

Fathers pass on to their children, even in adulthood, the gift of a legacy, which can be good or bad. Given the advantages my father afforded me, how can I not invest the same energy in my own children? It would be so unfair of me to see what he sacrificially did under difficult circumstances and not do the same for my kids!

We as fathers will pass on a legacy to our children. What kind of legacy do you intend to pass on? This ideal is prevalent in fathering literature. In my own research, I've studied how a man's perception of his experience with his own father influences how he sees himself as a father. According to studies, men either compensate for or adopt the behaviors of their dads, whether present or missing. Evidently, when children have a good, interactive relationship with their father, they too adopt these same attitudes with their own children. Reports verify this, demonstrating that men tend to participate in the same activities with their children that their father participated in with them.

However, there is a divergence in attitudes when there is not a good relationship, or when the father is not present. These men who lacked positive fathering either model this behavior with their own child, or become excellent fathers as they attempt to compensate for what they did not have as a child. The lesson is that although fathers do leave a legacy, one of blessing or pain, it does not have to be accepted. A negative cycle can be broken. Despite their own upbringing, fathers can still determine how they will interact with their children. If you had a poor relationship with your dad, or if he simply wasn't around, don't allow your children to feel how you felt by repeating the cycle.

CLARENCE'S CORNER

If you are already a father, have you ever thought that being a father is a lifetime job, because even your adult children will need you? How they need you won't, and should not, be the same throughout their developmental stages, but they will need you. You'll need them too.

How do you make this happen? The easiest way to make a mutually beneficial relationship a reality is by putting into practice what Jeff has shared with us in this chapter, which is to be actively involved in *every* stage of your son or daughter's development.

When your kids are infants, change their diapers; don't leave this job just for Mom or other women in the family. Changing your baby's diaper is also a bonding time because you will find yourself talking to your baby, which will help him/her to learn your voice and your touch. These are the first steps for your baby learning to love you, and later to obey your voice. Your touch will provide security for your baby. Yes, the mess and the smell associated with diaper changing are a small price to pay in exchange for your baby's love and trust. In addition to diaper duty, play with your kids. I had a fun time tossing my baby girls up in the air (and I always made sure to catch them). They loved it and usually laughed, even though it did make their mother nervous!

When they become toddlers, help your kids refine their walking ability, introduce them to numbers, the computer, balls, sports, read to them, and find other ways to interact with them. The more they crawl and walk, the more their minds develop, which will help them tremendously in school. Play an active role in their development. Besides, you don't want their mama to take *all* the credit, do you?

As they become older, listen carefully to them. Ask questions that require more than just a "Yes or no" answer and more of a meaningful conversation. The foundation you lay by simply listening to your kids will reap tremendous benefits when they are teenagers. Your involvement will make you the greatest influence in their lives, so it is your choice whether or not you'll take this role.

Remember, how you treat them as teens will impact your relationship with them as adults.

I can't stress this enough, but the key to building this relationship is *communication, communication, communication!* Communication is to relationships what location is to real estate! Within our communication, we must first listen carefully, then express carefully. It's not a contest. The goal in effective communication isn't proving you are right and your child or their mother is wrong. Your goal is *understanding.* Understanding doesn't equal agreement, but usually if people understand one another, they are often led to agreement. Understanding usually alleviates frustrations. What we say, how we say it, and when we say it, make all the difference in establishing a *safe place* in which your child, regardless of age, can approach you. Communicate in a way that the person who is listening can understand and receive it.

Some of you are saying, "I've never done any of that." That's okay. Children, even adult children, are resilient. The older they are, the more difficult it is to regain or establish trust, but it can be done! The key is persistence and consistency. Don't give up and don't get mad. If your child has lost trust, it didn't happen overnight, so rebuilding or establishing trust (for example, if you were an absentee dad) seldom happens overnight. Hang in there; things will change for the positive if you don't quit.

Jeff has instructed us on what to do and he even provided some great examples. All we have to do now is put his principles into practice with our children. Schedule your kids into your day. The key is **quantity time**, not *quality time*. Quality time **comes out** of quantity time! If you are married, after your wife, your children have to be your priority, above your job even.

I've done this with my girls over the years and amazingly they still love hanging out with their old dad. Please don't think I've been perfect. In fact, I'm far from it. When my girls were in elementary school, I was what you might call a "ghost dad," always gone, focusing on my career. One incident changed that. My daughters, Christina and Michelle were nine and Andrea was seven years old. I noticed one day that one of them began talking about me in the third person while I was in the room. Talk about a wake-up call! I heard it loud and clear! I realized that my girls were getting what was left over from work. They needed my best, which meant for me a career change. Less money, but more time with my girls saved our relationship.

Now that they are all in their twenties, I can tell you that the change was well worth the effort. They often call from college just to talk—what a gift!

WHAT DO YOU THINK?

(Questions to answer for yourself, with your father if possible, in a small group, or with your girlfriend/spouse)

- If you have children, how old are they?
- Did anyone explain to you the life-changing influence of being a good father and how to be one? If no one did, why do you think that happened?
- Have you noticed that you may have changed in how you father Your children? How so?
- Are you spending more time with them as they get older? Why or why not?
- Was your father a good or negative influence? How do you think this has affected you?
- How do you think your father has affected the way you father (if you have children)? Why do you think this is?
- If you have teenagers, how are you helping them to make consistent intelligent decisions? What are their consequences for bad/poor decisions?
- What is your strategy for the developmental stages of your children, starting at infant and moving into the adult stage?
- What positive skills or traits do you believe you are passing on to your children?
- If you are the father of an adult child, what is your relationship with him or her and why?

- What do you want your legacy to be with your children and grandchildren?

_____

_____

_____

_____

_____

_____

_____

_____

_____

_____

_____

_____

_____

_____

_____

_____

_____

_____

_____

FATHERING DAUGHTERS
CHAPTER 3

Protective instinct for many a father kicks into high gear when it comes to raising girls. I love the scene in the movie, *Bad Boyz II* with Martin Lawrence and Will Smith who both play detectives, in which they are at Lawrence's house when his daughter's "boyfriend" shows up to take her on a date. Lawrence answers the door wearing a tank top and Smith comes up behind him waving a gun, pretending to be drunk, asking this teenage boy a number of questions. Was this Hollywood scene way over the top? No question, but I would love to imitate that scene when a young man comes to visit my daughter, maybe with Clarence acting as Jordan's intoxicated uncle. Just image how intimidating it would be to meet your girl's dad for the first time only to encounter this tough, 300 pound guy, filling up the doorway, with prison tattoos on his arms. As a teen, I would have thought twice about bringing that guy's daughter home late or doing anything inappropriate with her!

PROTECTING & EDUCATING DAUGHTERS ABOUT SEX

Recently on the Christian radio broadcast, *Family Life Today,* the discussion centered on topics from the book, *Interviewing Your Daughter's Date: 8 Steps To No Regrets* by Dennis Rainey, president of *FamilyLife Today.* In particular, Dennis Rainey and Bob Lepine talked about fathers' responsibilities in setting limitations when their daughters begin to date. This broadcast focused on how to discuss sexual issues with your daughter, helping to alleviate the pressures she might feel from her peers for sexual experimentation. For example, Mike McCoy who was on this broadcast says he says, "'I want you to keep your hands and your lips off my daughter," when interviewing his daughter's potential dates. Some people may hear Mike saying that even holding hands is forbidden, not sure he is saying that.

Initially, I thought that his advice was a little overprotective, yet it made some sense. Teens do have a natural tendency to explore and take any activity a little further than originally planned. Dennis made this statement on the broadcast: "What I challenge young men to do is not the issue because my standards may not be your standards, but the issue is what ARE YOUR standards?" I do like the message of Dennis' book, *Interviewing Your Daughter's Date: 8 Steps To No Regrets.* One of our most crucial fatherly tasks is protecting our daughters. In more traditional societies, one of the primary roles for fathers is protecting their daughters' innocence (virginity). Fathers today should have a similar sense of protecting their daughters. Being a father of three daughters, I feel a strong need to guard my girls. I sometimes wonder if I had a son, would I would feel the same need to be as protective of him.

TREATING MOMMA RIGHT HAS LONG-TERM BENEFITS

My relationship with my daughters has long-term implications on their lives. I'm the first man with whom they have a relationship. My treatment of them sets a standard for how they'll expect to be treated by the boys they date. On several levels, for my daughters, I am setting the precedence on how they will relate to boys in general; specifically, how they will relate to boys with whom they may become romantically involved. In addition, I'm aware that their adult interactions in a romantic relationship with a man are heavily influenced by their relationship with me, their dad. Our father-daughter relationship may also dictate how successful my girls will be in their personal romantic relationships.

My influence extends beyond how my daughters and I interact, but to how their mother and I interact with each other as well. It is vital for my girls to see how a mutually beneficial romantic relationship is supposed to work. Having a great relationship with my daughters, but treating their mother disrespectfully, would be counterproductive. Even when Danni and I disagree and are mad at each other, I never disrespect her, especially in the presence of our daughters. Neither do I disrespect or belittle her in any of my discussions with our daughters.

If this ever were to happen, I am man enough to not only ask for my wife's forgiveness, but also my daughters' forgiveness as it is a huge disservice to all of them to act that way. My hope is that they understand that it is unacceptable when a boy or man disrespects you. A disrespectful boy isn't a candidate for dating and a disrespectful man certainly is not a potential marriage partner.

Most people seem to think that much of our actions are innate, thus so are our interactions with others in relationships. However, much of our ideas and attitudes in relationships are learned behaviors. Children often internalize behaviors of their parents and these behaviors manifest themselves in their lives. One way of protecting our daughters is by making sure we are providing the best model of masculinity possible. From their interaction with us, they will learn to have a higher standard of expectation for the boys, and later on, men in their lives.

My Presence Impacts My Daughters' Future

Empirical research highlights how girls benefit from having a positive and meaningful relationship with their dads. Fathers losing or abdicating their place in the family has a direct correlation to many of the social ills that our country is experiencing. Clearly, there is a parallel with issues such as teen pregnancy, risky sexual behaviors, early sexual relationships, abortion, and the absence of a father in a girl's life. Also there is substantial evidence of positive educational outcomes for girls who have an involved father. I must add that some literature has been critiqued because of the additional variable of income that is usually included in discussions involving fathers' presence or absence. For practical purposes, I contend that separating a father's financial support for his daughter isn't possible because if a father is physically and emotionally supportive of his daughter, then he is probably supporting her financially as well. Although men have different abilities to provide financial support for their children, rest assured that for most fathers, if they are in the home, they are being a provider.

Empirical research reveals the essential benefits for girls of having their fathers in their lives because fathers have traditionally served as protectors and providers for their daughters. Some research has focused on the effects of absent dads. For example, a study by Ellis et al. (2003) examined the effects of a father's absence on the onset of female adolescents' sexual activity and pregnancy. This study compared the difference in sexual activity and pregnancy among girls who had an early father absence, late father absence, and consistent father presence through adolescence. The findings suggest that teenage girls who had experienced father absence at an early age (less than five years), also reported an increased rate of sexual activity and teenage pregnancy before the age of 16. Girls experiencing later father absence (five to 13 years) also had increased rates of early pregnancy, but not as high as early father-absent girls. Another interesting finding was when girls experienced early father absence, they also experienced higher levels of life adversity factors, including low socio-economic status and familial conflict. These factors could potentiate the earlier onset of sexual activity and adolescent pregnancy, although father absence was still found to be a prominent major risk factor for early sexual activity and pregnancy in adolescent females. These authors concluded that adolescent females exposed to father absence, particularly at an early age, have a greater risk of engaging in sexual activity and becoming pregnant at an early age, whereas father presence proved to be a protective factor against early sexual activity.

Know Where Your Children Are & Who Their Friends Are

The research results do not indicate *why* a father's absence might increase the likelihood of early sexual activity and pregnancy, but let's not put the cart before the horse. Given that pregnancy is the result of intercourse, should we focus on early sexual activity among girls who experienced early father absence?

Referring back to the *Bad Boyz II* movie with the teenage boy visiting his girl's house when her dad is home, how might the scenario be different if he visits her with no father there and is greeted by her mother?

This reminds me of an incident in my own family when my father-in-law wanted Danni and her sister to give this guy coming to see their teen sister the once over. Evidently, he had previously visited a couple of times and Danni's dad wanted his older daughters to "rough him up a little by giving him the third degree." Danni had it all planned before she visited her parent's house to grill her little sister's new "serious" boyfriend. She even informed me that she was going to ask him what his plans were for her little sister and then follow up by informing him when he should return with her sister and inquire about where he planned to take her, among other questions of the third-degree nature.

This experience taught me that even when given the same intentions to be protective, men *are* different from women. After the young man was at the house for about five minutes, Danni and her older sister, supposedly the *bad guys*, were already commenting on how cute and well-mannered this guy was. For those boys out there that may come knocking on my door to pick up one of my girls, know that no matter how cute or well-mannered you may be (and you better be!), I will not call you cute or well-mannered when you are coming to visit *my* daughters!

Not only should we be mindful of who our daughters are interested in, but also who they hang around. But now it is tough! When I was a teen, when people called the house, a parent could get a sense of who was calling and how much time was spent on the phone. Back then, my dad had no problem picking up the phone to tell me he had to use it or he'd just plain tell me to get off the phone. Sure enough, I was in the middle of dropping some of my best lines when my dad would say, "Hey Jeff, I need to use the phone." Now I can't gauge who my daughter is talking to. It's all text messaging, and by the way, how persuasive can you really be by texting someone? I guess where there's a will, there's a way, and this generation has figured out how to communicate with their boyfriends while keeping us dads out of the loop. We still must be mindful of who our daughters' friends are as, friends they are extremely influential, and peer pressure can be detrimental. I figure if friends are going to have a major influence on my girls, then I might as well maximize my advantage by making sure my daughters hang around girls of whom I approve. They hang at our house and I know their parents.

Is Your Fathering or Lack of It Putting Your Daughter at Risk?

Farrell and White (1998) suggest that an increase in the level of peer influence is one of the implications of father absence. Their investigation delves into the association between adolescent drug use and peer influence, family structure, and family relationship. They suggest that father absence exposes adolescent girls to peer influences and adverse behavioral choices, and that fathers' presence may offer protection against the vulnerability associated with these choices. Their study found that peer influence was related positively to frequent drug use, particularly for adolescents from father-absent homes. The impact is more evident for adolescent females and those experiencing familial conflict. The reason a father's absence negatively influences girls' behavior and attitude is the subject of debate. Is it financial, lack of positive father-daughter relationship, or not having a father in the home that puts some girls at increased risk of sexual exposure? For whatever the reason, research shows that on average girls tend to have higher levels of at-risk behaviors when they don't have a positive relationship with their dads. As a result, it is imperative that fathers be there for their daughters. Much of the focus on fathering is the idea that it takes a man to teach a boy how to be a man. I don't disagree, but in this message, we must not forget how critical it is for us to also have a positive relationship with our daughters. There are also a number of positive educational outcomes for girls when there is a father present in her life.

Studies support the fact that a daughter's separation from her father may result in a risk associated with losing the masculine voice of morality and spirituality in the home. Children will eventually make life-long decisions, and with the absence of the father, peer and societal pressure becomes a significantly more powerful influence. From a human developmental standpoint, it is expected that adolescents will stray from their parents, and it is normal for peers to become increasingly influential. However, a father's presence can help to curtail or override many negative peer and societal messages our daughters are receiving.

Our daughters are inundated with media images of beauty and supposedly feminine behaviors. Think how many scantily-clad women we see on commercials trying to sell us something. And have you watched a Teen PG-rated movie lately? Based on what I've seen in the media, my next project may need to be on the negative sexual images media sends to our daughters. Our little girls internalize these images, wanting to be just like what they see on TV and at the movies.

I've been extremely energetic in contradicting the common stereotype of a teen female that focuses only on her external beauty by making an effort to ensure that my girls realize that their greatest asset is their intelligence. For example, I am big on math skills so we spend a lot of time working on math problems, discussing situations that involve complex math, and playing math games on the computer. To support my efforts, I inform their teachers that they need to be challenged in math. Why? Because as minority women, they are least likely to make it in a career that is math oriented, and careers in math usually provide tremendous financial compensation and career security. My focus on rewarding my girls for mathematical excellence is one way that I offer something to them besides what our society has dictated in regards to career choices.

Even though provider and protector have been established as the fathering role for daughters in western societies, this role is expanding to include nurturer and educator. Research supports that girls with active and engaged fathers have higher levels of cognitive ability than children without fathers. Critiques of this literature suggest these differences are due to socioeconomic status and dual parental attention, rather than father's influence. Regardless of the lack of controlling variables, the fact remains that your relationship with your daughter is beneficial to both her childhood, and later her adulthood.

FROM TOMBOYS TO GIRLS TO WOMEN

Relationships between fathers and daughters begin to decline as girls get older according to some literature. A segment of this qualitative data suggests this decline is due partially to the level of difficulty that comes to fathers in accepting the maturity of their little girl as she approaches womanhood. As a result, both may be apprehensive about discussing issues of dating, sex, and other topics which are at the forefront of a female adolescent's mind.

Fathers may also experience difficulty with their daughter's increased emotional makeup.

I'm grappling with some of these issues as my oldest daughter has recently turned 14 and I can attest to the sudden change in behavior. For a semester, I had to leave my family to teach at another university out of state and after being gone for approximately one month, returned home to discover my tomboy, who I could always find wearing sweatpants, was *now* wearing eye shadow! I remember looking at her as she passed me in the kitchen. "What is wrong with your eyes?" I asked her. "Nothing, nothing!" was her response. Well, I let it pass thinking it was the light hitting her face, but I noticed it again the next day and repeated my question, "What is wrong with your face? You look funny." My wife later informed me that she was now wearing eye shadow daily. Naturally and immediately, I inquired, "Where is she going that she needs to wear eye shadow?" Later, my wife privately reprimanded me, informing me that this is normal for girls her age to begin wearing makeup and cute jeans. Selfishly, I wondered what would become of the all the Gap sweats I purchased for her. Needless to say, I was stunned.

Never having sisters, I didn't realize what a major transformation it is from little girl to runway model. More importantly, why did it happen so fast and why did *I* have to experience it? I was hopeful she wouldn't begin this girly stuff until she was in her late twenties, when I was in a better frame of mind to handle it. However, I am proud to say that I have refocused, being proactive in my present situation, attempting to somehow re-figure or maintain our positive relationship. With her mother acting as the dominant force, I try to be the quiet still voice in her ear, but I need to move fast to maintain our relationship because scholars have found that fathers are less involved with their teenage daughters than their sons.

STAY IN TOUCH: EVEN AS WOMEN, OUR DAUGHTERS NEED US (AND WE DON'T HAVE TO HAVE ALL THE ANSWERS)

Studies of father and daughter relationships reveal that fathers feel a sense of uncertainty in their relationship with their teenage daughters. Your feelings of fathering a teen daughter are shared by countless other men in your predicament. The fathers who participated in these studies expressed feelings of uncertainty in their parental role. These feelings included, (a) deficient understanding of their daughter's "female" issues; (b) communication barriers involving topics and style of communication; and (c) limited involvement due to a lack of shared interests Nielsen (2001). The studies also highlight that girls tend to perceive a closer relationship with their mother than with their father. Nielsen (2001) reported that overwhelmingly, most adult women reported that their relationship with their mother was better and closer than with their father. Most of these young women reported knowing their mothers much better than their fathers and *most reported wanting a more emotional intimacy with their father*. The research also suggested that ninety percent of the women in the study claimed to be too afraid, uneasy, or tense to even talk to their fathers about topics other than "superficial" issues like school or money. Nielsen argues that most academic research on the family tends to downplay or ignore the father-daughter dyad and focuses instead on father-son interaction and mother-daughter relationships. Therefore, if the father-daughter connection is as distant and emotionally void as some claim, perhaps fathers simply are subconsciously responding to the parenting relationship in which they felt a stronger sense of efficacy, value, and positive influence (i.e., where he felt he performed best as a good father).

Even with the uneasiness, or lack of reported intimacy in the father/teen daughter relationship, one can still conclude that a father's presence is extremely vital to the well-being of his daughters. Although the research tends to support that the closeness shared between fathers and daughters in their childhood tends to wane as girls reach puberty, the relationship you establish with your daughter dictates a lot of the person she will become.

Additionally, it is comforting to know that most young women expressed that they wished to have a more meaningful relationship with their dads. This being the case, maybe we as fathers are at fault for allowing the decline in our relationship with our daughters over time simply because we tend to be uncomfortable with our daughters' emotional and physical changes. We as men must work at learning to better understand our daughters. Being more approachable and opening up more to them is a good first step. If we initiate those actions, we may decrease the level of emotional separation in our relationships.

CLARENCE'S CORNER

Our natural tendency as men, and one of our core values as fathers, is protecting our family—our wife, if we are married and our children. Honestly, I'd say fathers tend be much more concerned with protecting our daughters than our sons. Back in my teen years, there seemed to be a double standard of allowing boys to have sex (almost encouraged to do so as a proof of manhood), yet girls were not to have sex until they were married.

As fathers, whether we have boys or girls, we should educate and protect them regarding sex, the benefits, and abuses of it. The non-profit organization, *Think Marriage* (www.thinkmarriage.org) urges young adults to not live together prior to marriage. They say that moving in with your boyfriend or girlfriend as a "trial marriage" doesn't work. Recent research by the University of Wisconsin indicates that 40 percent of couples who live together break up before getting married. Additionally, couples who do marry after living together, experience a 50 percent higher divorce rate than those who didn't live together prior to getting married. Additional information can be found at www.twoofus.org.

As your girls grow up, they also grow *out*, making most of us fathers somewhat uncomfortable. We have no problem showing affection to our daughters before their bodies start to develop and they begin acting more like women. But once this happens, it can become quite awkward for fathers. We are no longer quite sure how to act. We begin to question if it's okay to keep hugging our daughters. We consider what now is appropriate and what isn't, and wondering how our daughters feel about it. Our girls may have adult bodies, but they still want our fatherly affection. After all, they're still our girls and our affection (not just affirming words, but touch) provides them with security. Most women want at least ten-twelve non-sexual hugs daily. This security will help them develop self-worth, so they won't go, as the old Johnny Lee song says, *"Looking for love in all the wrong places."*

Consider this scenario: A young girl, who didn't receive healthy affection from her father, went looking for love and found it (she thought) with a 43 year-old married man. She is now a mother with no father for her baby. This is not an uncommon situation.

When my girls were little, and even today when I leave the house, their mother always asks me where I'm going and when I'm coming back. Honestly, I used to resent this question because it conjured up memories of my own mother asking me the same questions when I was a little boy and teenager. Answering this question used to feel like a challenge to my manhood until I learned that it gave Brenda and my girls security. I realized that I could give my family, which I love, security by simply keeping my wife and girls informed of my plans. I also tell them I love them every time we end a conversation, especially with two of my girls away in college.

Dr. Gary Chapman has written numerous books, and two that resonate with me are *The Five Love Languages of Children* and *The Five Love Languages of Teenagers*. These books share how to determine your daughter's love language and how you can best love her in that language. If you are married, you can do the same with your wife.

This chapter is so close to my heart. For years, I heard, "When they (my daughters) become teenagers, you're going to lose them." Well, thankfully this hasn't been the case. In fact, it has been just the opposite. The older my girls have become, the richer our relationship has grown. They actually *want* more time with me! Michelle in college and now in law school, often says, "Call me or come see me." Christina, her twin, who attends a community college, lives with us. We try not to miss our weekly dad and daughter night at the movies (although, lately, it has been a little tough to make it because of her schedule, not mine). Andrea, who is in grad school, requests I call her weekly just to talk. We also Skype periodically.

How did this happen? With my girls, my wife and I began praying with them when they were about three. We also tried to have family devotions after dinner. These devotions happened fairly inconsistently, so don't worry about being perfect. I developed a "Girls' Night Out" when our twins were about three years old and Andrea was about fifteen months old. As my girls grew, I coached them in sports. They all knew how to correctly shoot a basketball on a small goal by the age of three. I stopped training them for a while because I didn't want to be a pushy ex-jock dad, but I regret it. In retrospect, I would have continued, not just because they would have been outstanding basketball players, but because of all the extra time I would have spent with them. I took up coaching them again in tennis and basketball when they were in high school. Michelle won the MVP award on her tennis team her senior year in high school and also served as team captain. Andrea qualified for State in track each year she ran, except her senior year when she was injured. Christina was the best three-point shooter of all the girls on the school basketball team, and more than held her own against college players during the summers.

Fathers, teach your daughters a skill of some kind because it is critical for their self-confidence. It helps them survive the brutality of middle and high school kids when they are so impressionable, and it keeps them from becoming needy or co-dependent on people or things. It has long been said that girls tend to seek a marriage partner who is like their fathers, so our investment in our daughters will influence who they marry and their quality of life!

Dads, you may find this to be painful, but you will have to watch more than your share of "chick" flicks in order to open up discussion about boys with your daughters. If these kinds of movies are good for anything, it is the conversations about boys, relationships, sex, etc., that can be generated by watching them with your daughters. It is essential having these kinds of conversations because they help you know what they are thinking as well as help increase their trust in you. One such conversation was with Andrea when she was 14. She wanted to go to a party with no adults chaperons. I said, "No!" We had a conversation about how boys and girls think. She was very surprised. She said, "Thanks for your insight, but you are cramping my style." A few days later, she says, "Thanks for not letting me go to that party. My best friend went and said the guys expected the girls to have sex with them. Thanks for keeping me out of that situation."

Christina, Michelle, and Andrea are all in their 20's. They still spell love "T-I-M-E." Girls are all about relationships and because of the time that I invested during my daughters' younger years, they now are at ease when it comes to talking to me about their bodies (often more than I want to), their spiritual lives, and about the boys they like or are dating.

Another reason for our closeness is because I would periodically ask my girls to evaluate how I was doing as Dad? Their first response when little was, "It hurts when you spank us!" My reply, "I mean for it to hurt. But other than that, how am I doing?" Sometimes, they would tell me I was too hard. I would evaluate and sometimes they were right—resulting not only in my apology, but a noticeable change in my fathering actions.

What Do You Think?

(Questions to answer for yourself, with your father if possible, in a small group, or with girlfriend/spouse)

- How are you protecting and educating your daughters regarding boys and sex?

- If your daughter is old enough, have you had the "sex talk" with her? If not, why?

- How would describe your present relationship with your daughter?

- How would she describe it?

- Does she talk with you about herself, friends, problems, et cetera? If she doesn't, why not?

- How are you treating her mother? How do you talk to her about her mother when she isn't present?

- Do you need to ask your daughter or her mother for forgiveness? If your answer is "yes," when will you do it?

- Do you have a regularly scheduled time that you spend with your daughter? If you live in the same house, this needs to be a daily scheduled time and don't ask "yes/no" questions.

- How are you handling your daughter's transition from your little girl into a woman?

- Are you continuing to give your daughter non-sexual hugs and kisses as she matures?

FATHERING SONS

CHAPTER 4

A LIVING, LIFE-LONG EXAMPLE

I don't have a son, but I was once a boy, maturing into a man with the help and guidance of my terrific father. He was always present and active in my brother's and my life. We currently maintain a great, healthy relationship. I am most proud of him because he fathered with the purpose of teaching us life's lessons, he rarely passed up an opportunity to find teachable moments every day. His lessons centered on teaching and reinforcing traits such as value, work ethic, and responsibility. My dad seemed to believe his most critical task as a father was to raise responsible men. He felt that if he put in the time, while we were young, to instill in us these life lessons, and he wouldn't have to take care of us as adults. He always made it clear that we would not be welcome as residents in *his* home after adulthood. Whatever the reason, he seemed to be intentional in his fathering, which is different from establishing a roadmap for my life. Under his guidance, he let me figure out my life's mission on my own. This was a journey that served as my *passage into manhood*.

Born to illiterate, poor, sharecropping, African-American parents in the South, my dad had all the odds against him. He grew up in unimaginable poverty, attended impoverished segregated schools, struggled with an undiagnosed learning disability, and had a child way too early in life. But I am proud to say he held strong as he never quit on his wife and kids. He is the epitome of the American Dream as he exemplifies how one can achieve his or her dreams through hard work and perseverance. There were often setbacks and disappointments, but he would just work harder.

From my perspective, the most indispensable character trait my dad has always shown in his daily life is in the fact that he never contradicts himself, or in other words he is not a hypocrite. I saw him practice what he preached. Recently, he had some financial setbacks due to the economy. He discussed his future plans with me. Even though he is a little older, his message was the same as it always had been; he will make it with a little hard work and sacrifice. He can recover all that had been lost. As an adult with my own family, my dad is still teaching me! Seeing him persevere through his recent ordeal has given me an amazing fathering model to follow as an example to head and lead my own family. We've got to hang in there as dads, because *giving up just is not an option*!

Much of who I am as a father can be attributed to how my dad raised me. This is known as "Intergenerational parenting." It addresses the phenomenon of fathering the same way that you were fathered as a child. A majority of the research on this topic has identified issues such as parenting attitudes and activities in which men tend to emulate their fathers with their own children. My research shows that fathers often participate in the same activities that their fathers did with them as children. Fathers often tell stories of helping their dad fix the car, spending time fishing, or hunting when they were children, and as adults these men find that they now duplicate these same activities with their own children. This is particularly true when a positive relationship exists between a child and his father. Some may jokingly come to the conclusion that these men (myself included) just aren't that creative as dads; rather than come up with our own thing, we repeat the fun things our dads did with us.

Speaking of fun dads, mine has always been a jokester. As I grew up, he would tease us and he left no one out; not even mom. We were always laughing at something he was saying or doing. As my brother and I got older, we picked up the same ability to verbally joust and come back at each other with quick-witted responses. My dad is known for never giving a straight answer and jokingly exaggerating some story, and now I find myself doing the exact same things with my girls. Rarely do they believe my first response when they ask me a question. Even the little one, Jadah will say "Daddy, really?"

Just as I perceive that my dad fathered with a purpose, I too am a big stickler when it comes to having all the girls do chores to teach them responsibility, so they can become self sufficient as they get older. Everybody has their duties and I am usually the one who enforces that these things are done. My dad's words echo in my mind when I chastise my daughter about playing outside before her chores are finished. I find that investing a little time into activities that will impact a child's future and instilling in them the priorities of life are the things you *must* do, and these activities take precedent over activities you *want* to do. Be deliberate in your fathering because most boys will imitate their fathers' parenting style. If you didn't have a positive relationship with your dad, you might compensate that by making a conscience decision to do the things with your child that your dad did not do for you.

Will You Be There?

A good friend of mine had a son out of wedlock when we were in college. He and his brothers were raised by their mother because their father was an alcoholic. He remembers the pain of his father abandoning him and the struggles his family endured because of that abandonment. This experience had such an effect on his outlook on life. Because his father was an alcoholic, he never drank while we were in college. Soon after graduation, he got a job about four hours away from his son, and he maintained a relationship with him despite numerous obstacles. He would call him every day. When his son got older and began playing little league sports, my friend would make the eight-hour round trip drive to see him play every Saturday morning! He would attend all the parent/teacher conferences and other events in which his son was participating. Eventually, my friend got married and had other kids, but he remained attentive to his oldest son.

He had shared with me early on how he wished his dad had seen him play baseball just once, and he went out of his way for his son because he couldn't stand the thought of him having an event or game without being there to cheer him on. Without accessing any statistical research findings, he realized firsthand the void he had in his life because of his father's absence in his life, and he made sure that void did not exist in his son's life.

Boys Without Dads May Never Grow Up

Earlier in this book, I discussed the effects of father absence on girls, but the effects of father absence may be far more pronounced with boys. Whereas a girl's absence from her father may be externalized, leading to an increase in outside influences because of the loss of her natural protector, separation from one's father may have more internalizing effects for boys. Some have theorized that the lack of positive father-son relationships might influence later adolescent aggressive behaviors, risky sexual attitudes, and poor school performance (McLanahan & Sandefur, 1994). The detrimental effects on sons growing up without their fathers' influence are also well documented. Compared to sons raised with a father, sons who grow up without a father are less likely to graduate from high school and more likely to be unemployed (McLanahan & Sandefur, 1994), are five times more likely to be poor, ten times more likely to be extremely poor (Nelson, 1995), more likely to engage in criminal behavior, become sexually active at an early age, and fail in their own marital relationships (Glenn & Kramer, 1987; Lykken, 1997; McLanahan & Sandefur, 1994).

I often question how much of the issues in the African-American community are the result of the lack of fathers in the home. Over sixty-eight percent of African-American children are reared in homes without a father. The African-American community might be a litmus test for what happens when numerous young men grow up without fathers. Although there are increasing reports of estranged dads in other communities, it is far more pronounced in the African-American community. Is this—gang activity, violence, and poverty—what happens to young men in a community that is void of fathers? My belief is that this is not the only answer, but one of many contributing factors which need to be addressed in the African-American community. Any effort to embrace young African-American men needs to start with them accepting their responsibilities as fathers. This will have lasting benefits to the community as a whole.

The father-son relationship has been found to be a significant predictor of a son's future communication behaviors (Buerkel-Rothfuss & Yerby, 1981; Fink, 1993), relational success, and communication with his spouse (Beatty & Dobos, 1993; Berry, 1990). Much of this can be attributed to the modeling behavior we have as men. Numerous men struggle with maintaining a meaningful, intimate relationship with their sons because they have never seen one. Simply put, they don't know how one works. If you were raised without a father, how might you learn what a father's role is in the family? Who do you ask? Where do you go?

Due to the fundamental nature of these issues, it is essential that you model positive behaviors when communicating with your spouse for your son's sake. Your son sees how you interact with his mother. When there are disagreements, it is vital for you to model for your son how to have restraint in conflict, yet resolve this issue without acting disrespectfully toward his mother. Your communications with his mother, whether you are married to her or not, teach him how to communicate with a woman and how to respect her. If you are a good communicator, then your son will likely be one also.

Research also reveals that boys with involved fathers have higher levels of academic achievement (Singer & Weinstein, 2000), educational attainment (Harris, Furstenberg, & Marmer, 1998), and income levels (Duncan, Hill, & Yeung, 1996). Many of these results can be attributed to a father's cognitive activities with his child. One argument is that a child growing up in a two-parent household has more adult interaction and resources than a child in a single-parent household. So much of this has to do with the extra interaction available to a child that has an active father in his life.

Education is another critical factor to be considered with father involvement. Although a simple equation, a father who is present and involved in his child's education bears a significant impact on that child's life. It is because of this impact that they must participate in their child's education. You don't have to go so far as homeschooling your child to be actively involved in his education either. It could be as simple as volunteering, holding him accountable for his grades, or helping him with his homework. I often volunteer at the school where my children attend and feel it vital for them to realize the value of their education.

Other areas that are affected by a father's presence are the potential for delinquent behavior and adolescent drinking (Simons, Johnson, & Conger, 1994), overall emotional health (Berry, 1990), and healthy attitudes toward sexuality (Fisher, 1987). Harper and McLanahan (2004), investigated incarceration among male youths from father-absent homes, and found that after accounting for the life adversity factors associated with single woman-headed families, including low socio-economic status, low education attainment, teenage motherhood, and racial inequalities, male youths from father-absent homes were at a significantly higher rate of incarceration compared with male youths from intact, dyadic family homes. These results suggest that young men who are reared under adverse conditions are less likely to participate in criminal activity when their father is present.

Dangerous and counterproductive masculine attitudes that exist in our country are adopted by young men without fathers. Many young men without fathers begin to identify with these unhealthy masculine ideologies because they lack fathers to help them navigate toward healthy masculine identities. Without their father's presence to provide positive, sensible and stable ideas of masculinity, they are much more likely to listen to peers and society's negative expectations.

My father helped mold my idea of what a man is by demonstrating the qualities that good fathers possess. Early in my childhood, I realized that being a father is more than just making a baby because I saw my dad as a provider, loving and honoring the mother of his children. It was also my first exposure to how romantic relationships between men and women work. My dad and mom disagreed and debated, but didn't argue. My dad was never physical with my mother when he was angry with her. I have seen him so mad that he left the house to go cool down, but he always came back in a few hours. These interactions taught me that sometimes you have to stand your ground, and other times it is okay as a man to back down. I also know that it is right to apologize when you are wrong, and that giving an apology, when it is necessary, is the manly thing to do. Having seen this model enacted in real life helped prepare me for my own marriage and parenthood.

We must be extremely careful with our sons as we model masculinity for them. Much of what is viewed as masculine traits by adolescents are not realistic models of masculinity. Taking care of your children, serving as a role model, financially supporting your children, and spending quality time with them should be applauded as masculine traits. All of these should serve as models of fathering. Most of the negative masculine ideas that exist are the result of fatherlessness in boys. A number of empirical studies highlight specific positive outcomes a boy experiences when he has a positive, caring relationship with his father. These studies suggest that these boys are much more likely to mirror their fathers parenting style, have improved levels of communication in every aspect of their lives, and have higher levels of emotional health and relational success in adulthood when there is a father presence in their life. (Simons, Beaman, Conger, & Chao, 1993; Simons, Whitbeck, Conger, & Wu, 1991).

GENERATIVE FATHERING

A final perspective for achieving an idea of effective fathering is found in what Snarney (1993) and others (Dollahite & Hawkins, 1998; Hawkins & Dollahite, 1997) refer to as "Generative fathering." From this perspective, effective fathering is framed by the enduring and repetitive cycle of perpetuating the next generation of fathers through the care and nurturing provided to the current generation of male children. Set against the obligatory or even socially mandated norms or expectations for today's father, the generative fathering framework emphasizes the specific type of activities fathers perform in response to the needs of their children. Fathering involves a genuine and even sacrificial sense of commitment, caring, and attention for a child's developmental processes; particularly for any biological sons who, in turn, will someday grow into fathers. Such fathering will ensure the survival of the family's bloodline and genetic material. In other words, your relationship with your son might affect your family for future generations!

My father viewed his role primarily as a provider. I remember many times as a child not seeing him for days at a time because of his work schedule. Growing up, I was often just with my mother and younger brother because my father worked so much, but his presence was there. We knew he was making sure we had our physical needs met.

As I got a little older, my dad and I began forming a much closer relationship through the time that I was able to spend helping him in his auto body shop after school and on weekends. As I recall, there were many late weekend nights that my father and I spent together at his shop. In retrospect, I probably wasn't much help as he often had to redo most of the things that I "fixed", but he was always patient, instructing me how to do it again until I got it right. During those times, we would talk about school, sports, or what he was doing to a car, and these nights in dad's shop gave us the bonding opportunities that have helped form the relationship that we have today.

As a preteen, he would have my mother drop me off at the shop to help him. There were numerous times when my dad would be using the loud sprayer to paint a car or banging on a fender, making it impossible to hear someone come in the door. On several occasions, people would walk into the shop and Dad could not hear them come in, so I proved to be a helpful "receptionist" in alerting him that someone was there. I thought it was always exciting to go to the shop with my dad, and I always felt cool when I could act as dad's lookout. During those times I felt I was needed and that I actually was a contributor to a greater cause. This was so valuable to my own self esteem and self worth, that my father trusted me—a little kid—to watch his back.

One fathering trait that I can trace specifically to my dad is that of provider. Another comes from his example of morality and spirituality, as my father was a role model for making moral decisions. For example, he not only insisted that my brother and I attend church, but he was insistent that we participated in church, and more significantly, he *took* us to church on a regular basis. These foundational teachings and practices were instilled by my father. I have not strayed from these practices and have tried to instill these same attitudes in my children.

Like all men, my father had shortcomings, and occasionally we had conflicts and disagreements. But I recognize much of who I am today—some good and bad—is a result of who my father is and my relationship with him.

CLARENCE'S CORNER

I'm nearly 60 years old and my dad, after all these years, *was* and *still is* my hero. I say *was* because he was shot and killed when I was 20 years old; at a time when I was trying to learn the meaning of manhood. My dad loved my mom, kissing her often in front of us. He had an eighth-grade education as my grandparents were poor, living on a farm with an outhouse back in the 60's in St. George, South Carolina. And as I mentioned earlier, he was a janitor for 38 years for the Reynolds Tobacco Company. And additionally, he was always working two or three just to support us.

As a man determined about making sure that his children were given opportunities he was denied, he decided that my sister and I *would* attend college. He valued our education and it was clearly understood that no "C's" were allowed in the house. If I brought a "C" home after the eighth grade, I was spanked, no discussion. I stopped bringing "C's" home.

I don't recommend this method, but my dad knew I had potential and with some things he didn't play.

My mom and dad belonged to different churches before my sister and I were born, but once we arrived on the scene, they joined the same church. In my family, attending church was mandatory, not optional. I remember hating going to church during football season because I wanted to see my favorite player Jim Brown, of the Cleveland Browns, play. Back in the day, we didn't have VCRs or TiVo so if I didn't watch a game when it aired, it was too bad. And Pastor Goodwin *always* seemed to preach until 1 or 1:30 p.m. I do believe that he preached into overtime each week just to make sure that I missed my beloved football games.

We weren't poor, we were "Po;" but I didn't know it until I went to college. We did everything as a family together. We were really close, making home a great and fun place to be.

I don't ever remember my father telling me he loved me, but I know that he did. My mom said it was because my grandfather, who was great with me, was not so nice to my dad, nor my aunts and uncles. My grandfather never told my father that he loved him either. It is difficult to say something you have never heard. It sounds strange, but in my years of counseling men, I've found it to be true. I was blessed to have a mother who was a student of my father.

My dad could play me like a fiddle. He was only able to see me play basketball in three of my games, and one of those three games was for a summer league All-Star game sponsored by the Harlem Globetrotters. My cousin, Mario from Buffalo, New York, was playing with us. He was a little fella, standing at 6'4, 240 pounds as a rising sophomore. We were losing, so my dad gets up and walks out of the gym. He returns as I'm laying the ball up to put us up by one. We won the game. On the ride home with my uncle and Mario in the car, I asked, "Dad, why did you walk out?" He responded, "I didn't pay good money to watch you lose." My mother later tells me he was watching all the time through the window in the gym door. He knew I wasn't playing hard, so he played me. I always wanted his approval and I worked hard for it.

I would win trophies and my dad would say little about them to me. It was my mom who told me how my dad would brag about me to his friends and acquaintances. Through my mom, I indirectly received my dad's blessing and praise. These indirect reports of praise that Mom gave me on Dad's behalf showed me that although he never said, "I love you, son," to me directly, he did love me and I was content with that.

I began preaching when I was seventeen years old. While away in college, my dad wrote me his first and only letter. This is what he wrote, "I saw a young preacher today. He reminded me of you. Keep the Faith." I read this letter over and over until the paper literally fell apart.

In some ways, I've never recovered from losing my dad so early in life, so I've adopted other dads and grandfathers. I still wanted my dad to help me understand, in his terms, what it means to be a man.

My dad taught me how to work hard and be responsible. He taught me that even though I can be extremely lazy, there are consequences to good and bad choices. Through his example, he also taught me how to treat a woman and remain faithful to her, and how to keep your word. As I've mentioned, he displayed a quiet dignity, even during segregation. I don't have that character trait. Maybe one of his greatest gifts to me was that he never crushed my dreams, no matter how silly they were. He never said there was anything that I couldn't become. And through his spankings that redirected much of my bad behavior, I'm sure he must have saved my life numerous times because—as much as I hated getting those whoopings at the time—they taught me right from wrong.

One thing I've done differently with my girls, than my father did with me, is to tell them early and often that I love them, I'm proud of them, and hugging them. I'm not blaming my dad because I'm not sure that anyone ever told him how much children need to hear this from their fathers. I understand that he never heard "I love you" from his father and that's why he never said it to me, but it was something that I longed for. In a way, he taught me the importance of expressing to your child that you love them. Through this longing to hear my dad openly express his love to me, I have been able to ensure that this longing wasn't something that I passed on to my own children.

WHAT DO YOU THINK?

(Questions to answer for yourself, in a small group or with girlfriend/spouse)

• Have you ever thought about how you father your son will impact your family to the third or fourth generation?

• What would be your one-word definition of your father?

• If your father was present in your home as you grew up, describe your relationship?

• If your father was an absentee father how has this impacted you? How do you think this affected your fathering? Or if you don't have children, how you think you would father your children?

• What are you doing to ensure your son's success in life?

• What do you think of the term, "Generational fathering"?

• As a result of reading this chapter, will you make any changes in how you father your children? Why or Why not?

• If your father did a good job in raising you and he is still alive, have you thanked him?

• If your father wasn't a good one, whether he is alive or dead, write him a letter expressing exactly how you feel. Then tear that one up and write him one that will not offend him. Doing so doesn't mean you will become best buddies, but it may free you up, possibly removing frustration and guilt, and ultimately helping you in your fathering. Forgiveness, which doesn't equal forgetting, is a powerful experience.

FATHER'S LEGACY

CHAPTER 5

Much of this book has been written to help the average father relate by putting empirical research concludes into layman's terms. Most men strive to be good fathers; however, the definition of a good father varies greatly. We should realize that most of us are limited by who we are and the examples of good fathering we have both experienced and witnessed. Until we step out of our own knowledge of good fathering and strive to know more, then we are hindered by our own definition of good fathering. This book's goal is to introduce those principles that have been demonstrated to be effective in fathering and explain how active father involvement benefits the child. I think all of us as fathers have a sense that we somehow matter and we try to contribute to the well-being of our child, but sometimes we aren't exactly sure how we matter or how to contribute. Now we know!

One topic that might not get as much attention as it should is how helpful fathers are to mothers in child rearing. Early research presents how a father's financial support benefits mothers and children by allowing moms to focus more on their children and family rather than providing. Of course, as many families need, dual incomes, much of our culture has moved from the dad at work/mom at home model, replacing it with shared income responsibilities between both parents.

Although many moms today are working outside the home, dads might be more necessary than ever in helping mothers than the earlier models of provider indicated. My own research discovered that a father's parenting attitude has an impact on the mother's parenting attitude. Much of the early research suggested that the influence was unidirectional in that it was just the mother's attitudes that influenced the father's parenting attitudes; however, recent findings suggest that, at least with cohabitating couples, the influence is bidirectional in that both parents influence each other's parenting attitudes. This is significant to know that fathers might intervene on their child's behalf in the case of mother's disciplining, deciding on chores, or appropriate activities for the child. Maybe we are finally moving away from the traditional notion that mothers are the gatekeepers of their children and it is their decision to allow fathers access to them. I don't think we have moved completely away from this concept, but maybe a shift is beginning.

In addition to influencing attitudes in a more practical sense, dads should lighten the load for mothers in caring for kids and managing the household. I was wired to do the "traditional" mothering activities in my house because my dad made sure we knew how to do yard work, cook, and sew. I saw my dad cook often, especially when my mother was in graduate school. He would come home, cook for us, and leave to go back to work. My wife is also accustomed to having shared household responsibilities as she grew up in a home where my father-in-law did most of the cooking and a lot of cleaning. In my house, I too do most of the cooking. While I am not very good at cleaning, I do what I can to maintain our household by doing things such as grocery shopping, hanging up my clothes, and running the vacuum cleaner. Hey, it's better than nothing!

Too many married women with children complain to me how their husbands cannot, or will not, grocery shop and cook. Now, I know that one of our greatest tricks as a man and a husband is to pretend we are unable to do certain things that we simply don't want to do. Our wives often buy into our act, resulting in our wives taking pity on us and doing these various tasks for us. I do realize that if a man allows his cooking, sewing, or shopping skills to be known, he will then have the burden of doing these chores from time to time.

One of my colleagues swears that on the occasions when she sends her husband to the grocery store, the only items he purchases are Twinkies®, Doritos®, soda, chips, frozen pizza, and Fruit Loops®. I laughed inside as not to "out" him. I know her husband doesn't eat that stuff; he is just perpetrating his inability to grocery shop. Instead of sharing with her my theory about her husband's game, I suggested that she send him with a grocery list. She said that she has tried that in the past and it hasn't helped. Now this dude is college educated, so I know he can read. This is just his way of fighting the system.

Another female colleague says her husband will always go to the store with her, but instead of helping her to gather items; he'll just push the cart. She then goes on to tell me that they've been married for five years and that he has always done this. Now, he's had plenty of time to learn how to shop. After all, if you watch someone do something for five years, you *should* be able to duplicate the activity. Even my ten-year-old knows how to grocery shop, so I imagine that this man is just going along to make sure she doesn't spend too much, rather than to take on the task of grocery shopping.

Dads really need to man up and lighten the mother's load. Choose one or two things that your wife typically handles and take care of it, or at least hire someone to do it. One of your responsibilities as a dad is not just to father your children, but also to assist the mother of your child. Mothers need more than just financial support from fathers. Providing care for the children by feeding them when they are young, or giving them a bath and/or putting them to bed will give mom a few minutes to herself so she can unwind.

I know that most mothers are gatekeepers when it comes to their child and if it is not done *her* way, then it is not the right way. But there needs to be some dialogue about your rights and wants regarding your child so you are able to lighten her load. I couldn't do hair, but I did help in other ways such as giving baths, helping my girls brush their teeth and putting them to bed most nights. Because of my work schedule, I often got my girls up in the morning and fixed them breakfast. Although they are older now, I still supervise what they cook (microwave) for breakfast, and help them pack their school lunches before taking them to school every morning.

Performing these tasks will help model fathering for your children. Your son will make a great catch for someone, and your daughter will know what to look for in a husband. Danni doesn't think it is extraordinary for me to go grocery shopping and come home to cook because she saw her dad do it. It was modeled for her. As you set this precedent, your generations of sons, and their sons, etc., will follow your directive and do these things in their households.

Not only should you take on some household chores, you should have some father and child time away from mom. You can bill this as a special night with your kids, either with just your sons or daughters. About once a month I try to take the girls to the movies, a ball game, or somewhere to give mom some time. In addition to taking all three of them, I also try to take them somewhere with me for one-on-one time. Jordan and I will catch a basketball game, Jiera will go with me to the store or to my office if I have some work to do at night, and Jadah rides with me to run errands—we will usually grab something to eat along the way. Taking my girls out on my own is a treat for them and a chance for their mom to sit at home or have some time to herself. At times, when I really wanted to earn some super husband points, I have sent my wife off to the spa while I've taken the girls for the day. Yeah, I am that good!

It's sad, but I know women who are fearful of leaving their children at home with their dads. We had good friends in Colorado who were like this. She could not go out of town without taking the two-year-old baby. The husband claimed the baby didn't like him, claiming that's why the baby always cried when mom left. In my opinion, it was a matter of having a spoiled child and husband. Mom spoiled the child because she never left her and dad was spoiled because he never had, nor did he want, the responsibility of solely caring for her. Part of being a great dad is trying to lighten the mother's load. One way this can be done is to take your children for half a day—maybe once a month—and let mom do her thing. While mom is taking a breather, take your kids to the movies, Chuck E. Cheese's®, the park, the library, or to the mall. Make it a monthly date!

Co-parenting

Co-parenting is one phenomenon that needs to be addressed in greater detail. Of course for children growing up in blended families, it is a necessity for all parents to be in one accord; however, not all children are raised in blended families. Instead, many of these children live with one parent, usually their mother, while their father resides elsewhere.

In most co-parenting arrangements, instead of nurturing a romantic relationship, the parents now must focus on establishing and maintaining some sort of amicable relationship to successfully raise their child. I strongly suggest that fathers take a proactive role early on in being a part of the child's life. Open, honest communication is the first step needed. The second step is for you and mom to reach an agreement that your child will benefit from having you present in his or her life. If you are able to establish this, then the mother (the gatekeeper) will allow you access to your child.

To avoid hindering your access to your child, it requires sitting down with your child's mother to draft some ground rules for your relationship as parents. First, men you have to either commit to or sever the romantic relationship, and all that remotely resembles romance, between you and the mother. *Translation:* this means no inappropriate remarks, flirting, and/or seducing of your baby's mother. These interactions further complicate an already complicated situation. Most women will struggle with your true intentions. You can say one thing, but if you are always trying to entice her, then you are doing another. Such actions will make it difficult for your child's mother to trust you. Leave it alone so you can fulfill your fathering role in peace. It's a lot easier to fulfill your fathering role in this situation if the mother doesn't have relationship expectations of you. I discussed earlier, you also should lighten your baby's mother's load. Do the things that are helpful to her. Research shows that she is a better parent when she has less stress. Helping her out will decrease her stress level so she can better parent your child and help her to trust you more.

When you are not residing with your child, it is crucial to DO WHAT YOU SAY. The mother will appreciate it and your child will respect that you are a man of your word. If you say you will call every night, call every night at a designated time and stick to that time. If that designated time is seven o'clock every evening, then call at seven. Not six thirty. Not seven thirty, but at seven o'clock each night. A child needs consistency and when you are not residing with your child, you have to be more vigilant in keeping this consistency in the activities with your child. Furthermore, **pay child support and pay it on time.** This action communicates loudly, not only to the mother, but also to your child. It reveals your character and integrity. By making it a priority to pay your child support on time, you are demonstrating to your child that he or she is your priority. Supporting your child doesn't have to stop at the court-ordered amount either. When possible, give more money for your child's upkeep. Most child support arrangements only cover the bare minimum that kids actually need. So when you are able to contribute more, do so. Kids know when you aren't giving your all. When they grow older, will you be able look them in the face and honestly indicate that you provided for them and cared for them to the best of your ability? Children can easily figure out that $250 a month is not nearly enough to care for a teenager, so you need to shell out anything else you can provide. The relationship that you build with your child through supporting her, as best as you can, will be well worth the sacrifice along the way.

Another key attitude in co-parenting centers on how well you treat your child's mother. Sure, you may have ended your romantic relationship on such a bad note that you can't stand the sight of her, but you must realize that it demands looking past your dislike for her and focus on raising your child together. This falls in line with the consistency issue. You and the mother must agree, as adults, that you have to do what is best for your child and any personal feelings must be put aside so you can be good parents to your child. You may be thinking "that is much easier said than done"—and it is,—but this has to be an attitude that you must embrace in order to be a part of your child's life.

I recently gave a presentation at a local church on co-parenting. Despite the fact that there were *plenty* of single mothers in the congregation who were invited to the event, the presentation was sparsely attended. The organizers were baffled as to why so many chose not to attend, so they started asking some of the mothers. They received numerous reasons why people failed to attend this event. Some women said that they no longer got along with the child's father and that it would be impossible to get him to agree to come with them. Others said that they chose not to attend since it would involve placing the child's father *and* their current boyfriend in the same room, which would be a recipe for disaster! One woman said that her current boyfriend would not let her meet with her baby's father. Another said that since her baby's father wasn't interested in attending a co-parenting class, she chose not to attend either. All of these excuses are legitimate issues that would have to be addressed in order to have a healthy co-parenting relationship and these issues can be resolved by the biological father.

If a healthy relationship does not exist between both parents, the father needs to man up by initiating the mending of the relationship with the mother. He needs to make it known to her that together they are going to co-parent their child until their child is grown. If the mother has a current boyfriend, the father needs to reassure the boyfriend that he is no romantic threat and that he is respectful of his baby's mother, her relationship with her boyfriend. Father needs to make it clear that he simply wants to participate in raising his child. Lastly, the father needs to be willing to set his pride aside and attend anything for his child that may involve him, his child's mother, and her boyfriend; yes, that includes co-parenting presentations. It makes much more sense that the father initiates these conversations as soon as he becomes aware his child's mother is in a relationship with another man to guarantee peace and that everyone is in one accord.

If I had a child who lived with another man, I would not hesitate to initiate any conversation with him. I would want to know who this man is and would need to get a sense of his morals and ethics. I would let him know that I would be around on occasions to check on and visit my child. I would communicate my expectations of him as an adult in my child's life as well as receive whatever expectations he would have of me as well.

We as fathers will certainly pass on a legacy to our children. The question is what type of legacy will it be? Will it be a legacy of modeling our behavior and a positive relationship, or will it be one in which our child will try to compensate for our inattentiveness? In my own work, I studied how a man's perception of his experience with his own father influences how he sees himself as a father. As stated previously, the results suggest that men either compensate for or adopt the behaviors of their dad. It is evident that when we have a good relationship and an interactive father, our children will also adopt these same attitudes with their own children.

There is a divergence in attitudes when there is not a good relationship or when there is no father presence. These men who lacked positive fathering either modeled this behavior with their own child or became excellent fathers in an attempt to compensate for what they did not have as a child. The lesson is that although our fathers left a legacy with us, one of blessing or pain, it does not have to be accepted nor continued. We can still determine how we will interact with our child despite our perception of our own father. Negative cycles can be broken. It is up to us to *choose* to do so.

It is noteworthy that a man's legacy of fathering is lifelong and generational. So many times we aimlessly go through life, or we put too much effort in our careers, not grasping the real long-term effect. I, for one, have gone through life anticipating the next big event, traveling plans, concert to attend, work project, or the next holiday. Although it is okay to plan out activities such as these, I also need to slow down to focus on my real legacy by being there for the daily things I do with and for my girls and their mother. Keeping my focus on them really puts life into perspective.

One way to view your effect on your family is to view it through the generative fathering perspective. From this perspective, effective fathering is framed by the enduring and repetitive cycle of perpetuating the next generation of fathers through the care and nurturing provided to the current generation of male children. We might expand the meaning of this concept by suggesting that one's fathering role is indispensable to one's offspring for many generations. Our fathering will influence the quality of the lives of our children, their families, and their children.

It is interesting to note that a man's fathering legacy is long-term and generational. If we operationalize family as a generational unit, then fathering becomes an invaluable mechanism of leaving one's legacy for future generations. As you think about your legacy, your role as a father may not result in having your name put in the ring of fame at the stadium, nor having an academic building named after you, nor will they have a "Where are they now?" television series about you, but your fathering influence is generational! There is so much negative modeling to which our families are exposed and your positive role as a father can have a tremendous influence on your children. Your sons, in turn, will adopt many of your parenting attitudes, principles, and activities. Your daughter will seek relationships that mirror many of your characteristics. She will love and respect you. Girls tend to marry men with the same qualities possessed by their fathers and she will be more likely to find a husband that has many of your parenting attitudes. As a result, this continuous positive fathering within your family will probably be traced back to you. Our fathering attitudes and activities become a point of reference for our children, their children, and their children.

CLARENCE'S CORNER

Jeff's Dad and mine are so similar. My Dad was a better cook than my Mom. His fried chicken was the best I've ever tasted—and I've had a lot of gospel birds. He also helped out with the household responsibilities. I never thought of him as being less of a man because he did. His role modeling for me has made it easier for me to help Brenda without the ignorant notion that it is "Woman's work." Brenda appreciates it too because her *love language* is acts of service. So helping around the house is like buying her flowers, only cheaper (she still likes flowers). My helping around the house also communicates to her that I love her. She has told me that my helping is a sexual turn on for her. Who would think that putting dishes in the dishwasher and running it is foreplay for my wife! Helping around the house also lightens her load so she can also have more energy and time for sexual intimacy. Now helping around our house isn't motivated by sex, but it certainly is one of the benefits with my wife.

Co-parenting has always been and probably always be something Brenda and I are constantly discussing and changing as our three girls mature. With all three being college students, with two living away from home, our parenting is different. Brenda and I communicate more with our girls as they are making most of their own decisions and living with their consequences. But Brenda and I have discovered that our girls want our input. They are responsible for their cars, etc. When they begin to date seriously, they bring that guy by the house, which isn't optional.

When I think of legacy, my prayer is my girls will marry a man who is a follower of Jesus Christ, faithful to her, a good financial provider, not threatened by her intelligence, and a lover of their children who will spend time with them.

WHAT DO YOU THINK?

(Questions to answer for yourself, in a small group or with girlfriend/spouse)

• Do you help your wife/girlfriend with household responsibilities such as cooking, cleaning the house and/or shopping for groceries? Why or why not?

• If you don't help with these responsibilities how do you think she would feel if you started helping?

• If you do help with household responsibilities, what do you think you are teaching your children?

• If you don't help with these duties, what do you think your children are learning from you and about you?

• Have you discussed in a cordial manner the importance of "Co-parenting" with the mother of your children if you don't live with them? Or if you are in a *blended family*, and the children are hers and not yours, have you discussed with your wife your role in "Co-parenting," such as discipline, child chores, etc.?

• How are you showing the mother of your child respect when you are with your child?

• If child lives with his or her mother and another man, have you gotten the other man along with your child's mother together to discuss each person's role in parenting your child? If not, why? What are issues you think need to be discussed?

• What do you think your legacy will be with your children? Do you think it will be different than you want it to be? It's not too late to make a difference.

ALTERNATIVE DADS: MEN *STANDING* IN THE FATHERING GAP

CHAPTER 6

STEPFATHERS AND OTHER FATHER FIGURES

Stepfathers and biological fathers alike know all too well how thankless their job can be. Despite the lack of praise that comes with this job, many men are stepping up to the plate and accepting the responsibility of becoming a father figure to a fatherless child. In my own work with fathers in low-income communities, I have met numerous men who served as father figures. Some were relatives to the child such as uncles and grandfathers. There were even instances where the mother's cousin was identified as a child's father figure. However, most of the men who were father figures held no biological ties with the children in their care, but instead were romantically involved with the child's mother. My relationship with my wife and, ultimately, the role that I have in Jordan's life falls into this category.

A lot of men would prefer to have no children involved, but quite often becoming a father figure is just part of the deal when developing a romantic relationship with women who are mothers. There are countless guys like me who now realize that most women in the dating pool have at least one child. Bearing that in mind, many of us accepted and welcomed (or at least expected) the responsibility of a child along with our new romantic relationships.

Numerous studies suggest that stepfathers can serve an integral part of a child's life. This of course depends on the relationship with the mother and the child's perception of the father figure. In the best case scenario, the father figure consciously serves as a father; he and the child both benefit from this relationship as a child would with their biological father. In short, the priority aspect is the *relationship* not the *bloodline*.

AFTER THE LOVE IS GONE: A CHILD STILL NEEDS A DAD

It has always bothered me when mothers who cycle through boyfriends every six to twelve months report that their *current* boyfriend is the father figure in their child's life. Children need consistency and consistent people in their lives. Change is hard for kids. Moms in the dating pool need to protect their children by not encouraging them to become attached to their short-term boyfriends. Moms shouldn't allow these boyfriends in the home unless they are "In love" or extremely "Serious" about the relationship. In turn, we as father figures need to be careful as we establish a relationship with a child. It is not just you and the child's mother who are becoming involved, but the child also. Even when the romantic relationship sours, do all that is possible to maintain your relationship with the child.

My cousin had a biological father from whom his mother was divorced, then, she remarried and divorced again. However, the man in the second marriage was always the father figure to my cousin. He was the man my cousin would call for advice because he felt the closest to this man. This man could have had the attitude that the end of the marriage was the end of his relationship with the child; after all, he wasn't his biological responsibility. Instead he took his role as father to another man's child seriously and maintained this very vital relationship even though my cousin's biological dad was around, but not involved in his life.

STEPFATHER & BIOLOGICAL FATHER WORKING TOGETHER

Personal experience allows me to confirm that being the father figure when the biological father is present has some difficulties. If both men aren't mature and sensible enough to dialogue to develop a co-fathering plan with each other and the mother, then numerous problems can and will arise. The child is the one who has the most to lose, often being caught in the middle of all the adult drama. When there are various romantic relationships involved, the men might have a difficult time getting on the same page, but it really needs to happen for the child's sake.

Jordan's biological father and I finally had "The Talk," not because we planned it, but because Jordan, then five, told him I yelled at her. We had this discussion in the parking lot at Jordan's school. He stepped to me and said, "Hey man, what is this I hear that you yelling at my baby?" Jordan was standing there beside her biological father and her expression told me exactly what she was thinking. "I told on you and my daddy gonna get you." At that moment, I could have felt threatened or even gotten macho on him and responded in a negative fashion. But instead I stood in his shoes, trying to imagine what he was thinking at that moment. Here I was this guy who he really doesn't know. We had only seen each other in passing up to this point and now his five year old baby girl was living with me and her mother. Given this shot of empathy, I decided that it was best to play it cool. I explained to him the circumstance in which I raised my voice at her and assured him that yelling at his baby was not something I did on a regular basis.

OUT OF WEDLOCK BIRTHS & DIVORCE RATES

Increasing out of wedlock births and the divorce rates have resulted in a drastic increase in children born without residential fathers. The Division of Vital Statistics (2009) reports that unmarried women account for forty percent of births in the United States. It has been reported that over 4.5 million children in the U.S are residing in fatherless homes and it is suggested that this figure will increase. The Division of Vital Statistics (2006) report that 69 percent of Anglo-American children and 55 percent of Hispanic children live in married or cohabitating families while only 27 percent of African-American children are reared in such environments. Although these rates differ greatly by race and ethnicity, it is clear that there are a significant number of children in the United States that do not reside with their fathers. The number of children being born to single mothers, along with the greater than 50 percent divorce rate, suggests a higher percentage of blended families today than there were just a few generations ago. It is inevitable that we will continue to see the increase of non-biological fathers or father figures in the lives of children.

The role of father figure sometimes becomes a little tricky as the biological father may still be present and involved in their child's life. Also, this father-figure may have biological children of his own so we're not just talking father figure, we're also entering step brother and step sister territory. When you consider all this change, it's quite a bit for some kids to process and accept. The issue of children's acceptance of this new parent along with a host of other issues has to be resolved in order to make blended families work to be a close family unit. I am revealing my age here, but the Brady Bunch did okay. In fact, they made it look easy. Not really sure how, but they all—even the maid, the butcher, and Jan for the most part—seemed happy and content. The Brady family did have problems, but they always seemed willing to talk it out and make sacrifices for the good of the family. Nevertheless, the critical influence of the fathering role is not diminished in these blended family situations. Even if your fathering role may need modification, your message and presence plays a significant and vital part in your stepchild's life.

With the dramatic increase in the numbers of blended families, more attention should be given to the men serving as a father figure to a child. Who are these men? Is there a specific profile that makes some men more apt to take on the responsibility of step-parenting? If being a parent is a thankless job, then you have to multiply that tenfold for step parents. Step parents spend endless amounts of time teaching, rearing and investing in someone else's biological children. When these kids receive the "Best kid" in class award with their name and picture in the paper, quite often the last name of that child—and the name that is recognized—is that of the biological father. Consequently, the biological father, whether he is around or not, gets some recognition of a job well done. Generations of your own family along with the general public admire great families such as the Smiths, Johnsons, or Robinsons. When you are a father figure to a stepchild, you don't automatically receive this recognition and your life-changing contributions might go unnoticed. As a result, when your stepchild's picture is in the paper for winning the local spelling bee and you choose to inform colleagues and friends that the child in the paper is yours, be prepared for a discussion as to why she has a different last name.

STEPFATHERING AIN'T EASY

Empirical literature discusses the difficulty that some men have in rearing another man's child. From a genetic or human nature basis, fathers protect their children, particularly their sons so as to protect their gene pool. Some naturalists would argue that it is the natural order of things. The natural order perspective or the Neanderthal view begs the question, "Why should a man spend his resources (time, energy, money, and intellectual capital) to benefit another man's gene pool." A number of theoretical studies on stepfathers highlight that this is a legitimate issue which cuts deep into human nature. Marsiglio (2004) attempted to understand the meaning and the negotiated identity associated with being a stepfather. This study found several interrelated issues as men attempted to father another man's offspring. The issues of timing, mindfulness, propriety work, naming, seeking recognition, and biological children serve as possible barriers for effective stepfathering.

Issues of being a stepparent are legitimate, particularly as you attempt to figure out your role in your stepchild's life. Of course, the natural role of father includes being a provider, disciplinarian, playmate, and moral teacher. The issues of discipline may be a volatile subject because the non-biological father might dictate discipline practices and a mother may desire some limitations on this role. I have always attempted to put myself in my stepdaughter's biological father's shoes. What if my two biological children were residing with another man? What would my expectations be of my children residing with him and then of him as a father figure?

I was blessed as a stepfather to have a fairly good kid who has given me no trouble as of yet. (She hasn't quite hit the "mean teens" phase so we shall see). My role as a disciplinarian has centered on my restricting her privileges on a few occasions and adding to her list of chores. Until now, my attitude has been for Danni to handle any serious issues if they arise. I figure that it is more trouble than it is worth for me to get involved with major discipline infractions, so I usually just stay out of it. Now I don't leave Danni on her own when it comes to difficult issues. I do chime in, giving my opinion of what should take place. I have even talked to my stepdaughter about issues after the fact. There have been times when I have had to discipline her about certain behaviors as well as laying out expectations for her as any parent would. But usually, I leave it between her and Danni. If I don't think it is being dealt with appropriately I discuss it with her mom in private.

Another tricky issue is that of the provider role. Although there may be issues with my disciplining Jordan, nobody seems to mind when I provide for her. Once when her biological dad was visiting at an out of state basketball tournament during the summer, she needed some money for a team event. Although her biological dad was there, she came to me for the money. "Dad, I need $50 for ..." My initial reaction was the same as always, digging into my wallet while complaining that they all only come to me when they need something. (It's a trend that my family has noticed, but I do tend to complain every time I have to go into my wallet for any of them; mother and daughters included.) As I was pulling out my hard-earned cash, the thought crossed my mind, "Isn't your (bio) dad here? Why aren't you hitting him up?" But I kept my thoughts to myself and shelled out the money anyway.

Treating all my children equally is a foundational principle for me. Whether shopping or in their general upkeep, I strive to be economically fair among all of my children. When assigning chores or tasks to ensure that they're "earning" the money that I'm handing out, I first make sure they are *age* appropriate as well as being fair. One issue that the literature discusses is the use of limited resources and the fairness to *all* of your children, biological or not. Though I'm not poor by any stretch of the imagination, there is a limit to the resources to which my children have access. If we expand these resources to include not just finances, but intellectual capital, and time, then it becomes easy to see that there is only one of me. Even if I had a bank account resembling that of Bill Gates, his day still only consists of 24 hours, like mine. Revisiting the naturalistic point of view expressed earlier, what is the benefit of sharing these limited resources with another man's child and in turn limiting the amount of resources allocated to your own child?

Hopefully we have evolved beyond being *Neanderthals*- basic human instincts and can rationalize the need to care for a stepchild in the same manner as our own biological child. In this context, we have a number of human instincts and have attempted to weigh the consequences of acting upon them. When confronted with this natural response, I have relied on my relationship with Jesus Christ in trying to answer these basic questions. Trusting and accepting that God has placed my stepdaughter in my life for a reason, I believe my fathering is serving a purpose in her life. Although I am sure I will eventually fall from her family tree, I know my role in her life as spiritual leader, provider, and disciplinarian will benefit her and her family's legacy for generations to come. As mentioned earlier, research shows numerous positive long-term outcomes for girls with caring fathers in their lives. I must intentionally bless and protect this precious gift God has placed with me! I must love and nurture her so she may be successful in life.

Having interviewed a number of men raised by stepfathers, many of them reported having a troubled, or at the least a distanced relationship with their stepfathers. However, many men raised by their biological fathers report having these same issues. A large number of men who had a stepfather reported fond memories of their stepfathers. Scores of these men said that not being treated like a stepchild or referred to as a stepchild was invaluable to them while growing up. This relates to the issue of how biological fathering is the benchmark. Step-children say that it is critically important for them not to be treated any differently than the biological children in the home.

Being a stepfather has been fairly smooth for me, although I do wish there were things that had been done differently. Just as the saying goes, hindsight is always 20/20, but if I could do it over again, I would have made sure that sure that all the adults had met together when our co-parenting responsibilities for Jordan began so we could discuss each other's expectations and how we would *all* raise Jordan. Her biological father and I have been cordial ever since our parking lot talk. Keeping him current on what is going on with her emotionally, physically, spiritually, and with her sports by sending him film and discussing her games etc., is my responsibility. We often sit in the stands together during her games, talking about her athletics. I wonder if it's strange to people to see her dad and stepdad coaching her from the stands. He has learned over the years that I can be trusted and that I love his child as much as he does. Respecting him as her biological dad is another principle I have learned. It is not his fault that he is unable to reside in the same place as her. He is trying to make the best of a complicated situation. My question is who will walk her down the aisle at her wedding?

CLARENCE'S CORNER

As I have previously mentioned, my father was robbed, shot, and killed when I was twenty years old when I was at home in Winston-Salem, NC on Spring Break. At the time, I was attending Moody Bible Institute in Chicago, a much more dangerous city than Winston-Salem. It's strange to see that no matter where you are and however safe you may feel, dangerous situations still exist. I lost my dad in 1974, but I still miss him. After Jesus Christ, he is still my hero. I find myself wanting to ask him so many questions about himself, my grandparents, how he dealt with social injustice and racial tension that he faced with so much dignity, parenting, my mom and their marriage. I know that he would have loved playing with his grandchildren and they in turn would have loved playing with him. His wisdom would be invaluable for my family. Today he should be filling the role as the wise patriarch of our family, but instead he is gone. Growing up, with him around, despite my age, I felt that I could still be a "Little boy," in some ways not having to grow up. When Dad died, that all changed. I became a man that day, having to take care of and trying to protect my mom and sister, Jean, who was a real Daddy's girl.

God has graciously given me Dr. Gary Chapman as my alternative Dad long before he became a *New York Times* best-selling author. He has always been there to encourage me, even when I flunked out of college. And he encouraged me when I made all "A's" my first full semester in graduate school, saying, "I knew you had it in you, but it is nice seeing it in black and white." I'll never forget this man literally running through a restaurant in Winston-Salem, North Carolina shouting, "Look at my grandbaby!" You should have seen all of those people looking at him. He wasn't ashamed to claim Christina, a black baby, as his own. He even did the premarital counseling for Brenda and me and he was my Best Man for our wedding. He is always there to give me advice, spiritual, and financial support when I ask for it.

God has actually given me several alternative Dads. The late Dr. T.B. Maston, Professor of Christian Ethics, Emeritus of Southwestern Baptist Theological Seminary. And there is John Bass, who taught me how to do consulting and continues to teach me about mentoring. Bob Cook has actually called me his "other son" and at times, I've called him "Dad." He has taught me much about marriage, family, legacy, and God. He has cried with me through difficult situations. And he has cried when he has had to tell me things I didn't want to hear, but needed to hear as any father who loves his son does. Dr. Don Sharp, pastor of the Faith Tabernacle Baptist Church is another alternative dad. He shares his life with me; the good, the bad, and the ugly. As a brilliant thinker and communicator, knowing he is always there is comforting. Dr. William Pannell continues to impact me by simply calling periodically to encourage me. Dr. John Perkins brought me to tears once simply by telling me he was proud of the way I handled a situation. He has served as a great source of encouragement in my life. Internally, I still want to please my father and it seems these men emotionally and subconsciously represent my Dad to me.

All of these alternative dads have dramatically changed and improved my life. Most of my success spiritually and business wise can be linked to these men. I can't imagine surviving life without them, especially as a husband and father. My wife and children will testify to this. I believe all men; regardless of background desperately need an alternative dad if our biological father isn't available. We need such an influence in our life, even as grown men, even if we have our own family. Jeff constantly mentions the ongoing influence his father continues to have on him. Dads need to realize that fathering does not stop the day that your child moves out of the house. Men need to seek elders for guidance and that's where father figures foot the bill.

WHAT DO YOU THINK?

(Questions to answer for yourself, with your father if possible, in a small group, or with girlfriend/spouse)

- If you have had an alternative dad(s) in your life, how did he/they impact your life?

- What do you think of this concept?

- If you are a stepfather or another form of alternative dad, what are the difficult obstacles you face in your efforts to serve effectively in this role?

- If you are a biological father, stepfather or some other form of an alternative father, how is the relationship with the other father, whether biological or alternative, working out?

- If it is not presently working well, what can you do to make it better?

- Are you willing for the sake of your child to work and have patience with the other man in your child's life?

- Have the two of you had a meeting with the mother to devise a mutually beneficial practical plan for raising your child together? Why or Why not? This needs to be done for the sake of the child, who desperately needs all of you.

- How do you "Thank" your father, biological or alternative for what he is doing in your life if he is still alive?

- If you were born out of wedlock, how do you feel this has impacted you?

- If you were born out of wedlock, what kind of relationship did you or do you have with your biological father?

- If it wasn't/isn't a good relationship, how to you intend breaking this "chain of pain" with your children if you have any?

- What have been some of the blessings of being an alternative dad?

- Is there anyone to whom you need to be an alternative dad?

_____

_____

_____

RELIGION'S *IMPACT ON* FATHERING
CHAPTER 7

Phil Jackson, Pat Riley, and the late Red Auerbach; none of whom profess to be particularly religious, yet all of these men used the biblical principle of *selflessness* with their teams to win a total of 22 NBA Championships! The late John Wooden, Dean Smith, and Roy Williams, all college coaches and men of faith, used—and still use—biblical principles in their basketball programs, resulting in multiple NCAA National Championships!

What I find so amazing is that beyond the championships are the relationships of love and respect many of the players, as grown men, have for these coaches who often served as alternative dads to them.

So if all of these men, some religious and some not, successfully used biblical principles for such a temporal goal as winning a basketball championship, consider the significance of using religion and faith as a father who is seeking to positively influence his child for a lifetime.

The previous chapters of this book have examined research literature to understand the effects of fathering on children from various developmental stages. An additional area that should be discussed is how our religious beliefs influence our fathering behaviors and attitudes. Or more specifically, how should one's religious beliefs influence how they father.

To this end, my friend and colleague, Dr. Clarence Shuler, was invited as a guest expert to aid in exploring the concept of religion, specifically Christianity in fathering and how it either confirms or contradicts the fathering principles found in the research literature. Regardless of your religious beliefs, this following section will be informative and may also expand how you view yourself as a father. This chapter is different in that the motivations to father differ in their rationale. Yet, it is believed that the outcome will remain consistent: educating men on their indispensable influence in their child's life.

Following is Clarence's perspective on religion's impact on fathering:

I am honored that Jeff has asked me to assist him by providing Christian principles based on my study and experience in this field. The Bible teaches the necessity and priority of fathering. This is obviously evident given the fact that the word *"father"* appears in the Bible over 1,500 times! This chapter will focus on the intersection of Christianity and fathering.

The Bible is relevant to real-life fathering as numerous positive and negative examples and models of fathering are found within its pages. Why give negative examples? Well, most of us learn more from our failures than from our successes and the Bible is confident enough in itself to provide some negative examples of what fathers shouldn't do. Through these depictions of fathers, we can learn a great deal about the roles of fathers and the consequences of good, and poor fathering.

In answering the questions presented in the study regarding the impact religion has on fathers, this chapter will parallel the research presented earlier in this book with one major difference. The difference is that the Bible will be used as a guide or resource book, filled with instructions on fathering.

SOCIETY VALUES RELIGION AS A PRIORITY FOR FAMILIES

During a January 2005 airing of the television game show, *Family Feud*, the audience listed the following as ingredients that hold a family together in this order of priority: trust/honesty, communication, love, r**eligion/faith**, children/family, and money. Isn't it amazing that a game show audience lists religion/faith as an essential element of a successful marriage and/or family? Note that this group of people placed religion/faith fourth in this list, *ahead* of children/family and money. If religion/faith helps marriages and families, then a natural conclusion is that religion/faith will help *all* relationships, including the relationship between father and child.

Dr. Ron Jenson, President of Future Achievement International and author of *Achieving Authentic Success*, says, "*Faith* is essential for any successful individual." So if faith is essential for any successful individual, then it seems that faith is essential for successful fathering and marriages.

FATHERING SEEMS INCREDIBLY DIFFICULT

I asked my alternative dad, Dr. Gary Chapman, if fathering is hard. Read his answer:

"Fathering is one of the most difficult endeavors, largely because it is personal and daily. Children have personalities and often Father's patterns of teaching and responding do not match the personality of the child. Thus, there are clashes of the will. Most fathers are not trained in anger management. Thus, they often mismanage their anger and deeply hurt the emotional development of the child. I think lack of information on discipline and anger management are two of the bigger issues.

If I could do it over, I don't know that I would do it differently. I'm not saying I was a perfect parent, but I did try to listen to my children and I sought to grow as a person when I realized that I needed growth. I enjoyed every stage of their development. It is extremely satisfying to see both of them committed to Christ and using their abilities for His glory."

Dr. Gary Chapman
New York Times Best-Selling Author of The Five Love Languages

BIBLICAL DADDY BASICS

You'll see quite a few similarities between non-religious fathering data and the religion of Christianity regarding the basics of fathering. But let me prepare you; some of the Christian data may pleasantly surprise you!

LOVE YOUR BABY'S MAMA

Loving your baby's mother is the second priority in biblical basics. The first, and most crucial step, comes later. How you treat your child's mother will drastically impact your child and their future romantic relationships, either positively or negatively. Remember, children do more of what they see their parents do, rather than what they hear their parents say. What are you communicating to your children by how you are treating their mother physically and verbally? Do you want them to repeat your actions or words in their present or future relationships?

Historically, many Christians have erroneously used Ephesians 5:22-24 to justify controlling, or in some cases, dominating their wives.

"Wives, be subject to your own husbands, as to the Lord. For the husband is head of the wife as Christ is also head of the church, He Himself being savior of the body. But as the church is subject to Christ, so also wives ought to be to their husbands in everything (everything honoring God)."

Unfortunately, it seems that verse 25, which says, *"Husbands, love your wives, just as Christ also loved the church and gave Himself up for her,"* is often overlooked. Christ becomes head of the Church by dying for the Church. So, headship for a man in a family is more about giving and serving than getting. If he serves well, usually, he'll reap the fruits of his labor for years to come from his wife, children and grandchildren. Servant-leadership, not dictatorship, is a biblical daddy basic principle. Are you willing to die for your family and to sacrifice for them? If you are, then living for them is easy and it is a choice you make every day, all day long.

Husbands in verse 25 are *'commanded'* to love their wives, which isn't optional. What does God mean here by love? If you study the second book in the New Testament section of the Bible, which is the Gospel of Mark, in chapter 14:32-36, your research will reveal that biblical love is not an emotion, but an action. Which is why Jesus Christ, in Luke 6:35, commands Christians to love their enemies saying,

"But love your enemies, and do good, expecting nothing in return; and your reward will be great, and you will be sons of the Most High; for He Himself is kind to ungrateful and evil men."

Jesus Christ Himself overrode His emotions regarding His pending death and obeyed His Father by an act of His will, allowing the Romans to beat Him before crucifying Him on the cross. So biblically, you can't *fall out of love.*

This is radically different than what society has led us to believe. Probably every married couple could file for divorce on the grounds of incompatibility since men and women are so different. But biblical love is not about **compatibility**, but **commitment.** You may have heard someone say, "I don't love her anymore." This person is expressing an emotional love often attached to past or present circumstances with unhealed wounds. He is not looking at life's "big picture" for himself or his children. One of God's foundational expectations of a positive, effective father is that of marrying and loving the child's mother, preferably before the baby is born. Of course, it can still work if you have married the mother after the baby's birth, too.

Ways to Love Your Woman (And She'll Love You for It)

Real men help clean the house. This models positive behaviors for sons by showing them that, rather than just sitting on the couch watching ESPN while their wife keeps the house in order, they too should help around the house. On the surface this may seem like a bad deal, but believe me, this can be very rewarding. A man who helps around the house will be attractive to women looking to find a life-long husband. In the long-term, such a man will leave a positive legacy with future generations of his family. But this also has one short-term benefit that can be quite rewarding. In helping out, he'll make his wife happy, who in turn will return the favor in, ahem, *other* ways.

HELP WITH YOUR KIDS

Another way of loving your woman is by helping with parenting. For example, you could help with your children's homework, but only if you are smarter than your children. Not all of us are good at helping our kids with their homework. If you can't, that is fine. Let your wife help your kids do their homework while you clean the kitchen, which is another way to lighten your wife's load. Lightening her load is a way of telling your wife that you love her, so find ways to help out where you can.

SHOW HER THE MONEY

Most wives want their significant others to show them the money by paying the bills—*preferably on time*—and by being the primary breadwinner. Now, not all men work in professions which allow them to be the primary breadwinner, and if your wife makes more money than you, consider yourself *blessed.* It doesn't make you less than a man because she earns more. In the end, you are both teammates, not competitors with one goal in mind: providing for your family. Providing for your wife and family gives your wife security.

GIVE HER "ME TIME"

Giving mothers a little time off here and there is another example of lightening a mother's load. We fathers need to schedule regular times to take our children out to play, the library, special sights in the city or anywhere for a little day with dad. By doing this, we are giving our wives a few hours to relax and focus on herself for a little bit. Send her to the spa, the salon, or send her off with a gift card to her favorite store. Whatever your means, and whatever her taste, the point is that you give her some "Time off" from her duties. Give the mother of your child something to look forward too. Your thoughtfulness will go a long way.

Even if you are no longer romantically involved with your child's mother, you should still do this. If you give of your time so she can have a little time for herself, she will be more likely to speak positively of you to your children when you're not around. She deserves it. Remember, she is still mothering your child.

BE MR. MOM (SOMETIMES)

Often mothers wrestle with daily cooking duties. Whether it's coming up with a creative menu that Jr. will actually eat, having the time to cook, simply keeping the kitchen clean, or feeding the family can really wear on a mother. Now, this may not seem like a big deal to most men, but it's a huge source of stress for women.

As a father, we have the tremendous ability and influence to strongly encourage our children to have daily responsibilities in the kitchen and around the house; building character and a good work ethic in the process. And the children can make a game out of coming up with new meals. Fathers, we can help cook, or at least help plan a meal or two weekly. If anything, we can pick up a few ingredients from the store on our way home! Okay, maybe you aren't going to cook, but all of the above make your wife's load lighter so help in whatever way you can.

BEING PRESENT FOR YOUR CHILD'S BIRTH

Even if you are not in a romantic relationship with the mother of your child, you should be with her when she gives birth. The Bible tells how Abraham was with Sarah when she gave birth to their son. Abraham named his son Isaac and circumcised him on the eighth day after his birth. Joseph was with Mary as she gave birth to Jesus Christ according to Luke 2:4-7, 16. So Joseph, the "father" with his newborn is being supportive of Mary, the mother of Jesus. He probably helped with the delivery since they weren't in a hospital, but rather a cave used as a barn. Joseph's influence on Jesus is seen in that Jesus is called the son of a carpenter, which was Joseph's profession (Matthew 13:55).

In the Bible, fathers were there with their wives for the births of their children. Jesus, in Luke 18:15, encouraged parents to bring their babes, which can be translated as children, to him. He touched them.

A man's touch is so crucial for babies! Recently, I experienced this. My wife is so gracious to help young mothers by watching their babies so they can have a little time to themselves, or so both parents can have an occasional date night. Once she agreed to babysit a baby boy, who was less than two-years-old. Naturally, my three daughters were all over him, but once I entered the room, this baby boy was fixated on me. And once I picked him up, he only wanted to be held by me. I believe a man's involvement with his baby is critical. An excellent first activity for a father is to be present with his wife as she gives birth to their child. Such an event can bond the father with the mother and with the child. It's definitely not an event to be missed.

CHRISTIAN FATHERS ARE NURTURERS

"For you know that we dealt with each of you as a father deals with his own children, encouraging, comforting and urging you to live lives worthy of God". 1 Thessalonians 2:11-12

These verses demonstrate that we are not just role models, but we as fathers are to be nurturers and a source of encouragement to our children as well. Some men erroneously think nurturing is only done by women. But nurturing children is one of a father's most critical roles. It is a powerful life-changing opportunity and responsibility for a Christian father. Our children often see our hard side, but they need to see a man's soft side too. Nurturing, or lack thereof, will forever determine how our children see themselves because it affects their perception of themselves as they grow into adults.

FATHERS AS EDUCATORS

"Hear, O Israel: The Lord our God, the Lord is one. Love the Lord your God with all your heart and with all your soul and strength. These commandments that I give you today are to be upon your hearts. Impress them on your children. Talk about them when you sit at home and when you walk along the road, when you lie down and when you get up. Tie them as symbols on your hands and bind them on your foreheads. Write them on your the doorframes of your houses and on your gates." Deuteronomy 6:4-9

According to this passage above, God is telling (commanding) fathers (because this is a dominant male culture) to teach His principles to their children. Fathers are to teach these godly truths by talking with their children when they sit at home; implying fathers need to be at home interacting with their children before the children go to bed. The "sitting" could be in Dad's favorite chair, or with Dad sitting at the dinner table with the family, or Dad helping his children with their homework. And as I said before, if you can't help with their homework, let Mom do it. Show your children that a "real man" helps his wife around the house. You'll help your children by modeling for them the kind of spouse they should marry. Girls tend to marry boys with traits similar to their fathers because that is what they have seen modeled and that is what they are used to. Fathers may teach godly principles when they *walk* and spend time with their children.

What a blueprint this passage is for fathers, mothers too! Basically, it encourages us as parents to use every aspect of life as an opportunity to teach our children about our faith. Parents are instructed in this passage to have biblical teachings and verses written throughout the house, so the children learn them not only by hearing, but by seeing them daily, as well as by observing their parents living these commandments. It is out of this quantity time that quality time is produced. Here's how you can follow this blueprint in your own home:

- Put important messages, such a verse of scripture, or principles by which to live, out in places that are commonly visited in your home. This could be on your refrigerator, your child's mirror, or maybe in your home's entry way.

- You might even want to have these messages outside the house as well. This could be on your doormat so they can be seen by all who enter your home (check with wife **first** if married).

- Memorize a life-affirming principle or a Bible verse with your children. It is a tremendous bonding exercise, as well as an effective mental exercise, which can result in academic benefits. And since children do model their parent's behavior, they will in turn teach this to their children.

Ephesians 6:4 says, *"Fathers, do not exasperate your children; instead, bring them up in the training and instruction of the Lord.* Colossians 3:21 says, *Fathers, do not embitter your children or they will become discouraged."* These verses reveal the positive or negative influence a father can pass on to his children and the power of a father's presence. The terms *exasperate* and *embitter* carry with them the idea of fathers wearing their children out because that child's best is never good enough. For example, if your child hits a single in a baseball game and you say, "You should have stretched it into a double," they may conclude that their best is never good enough so there's no use in trying and quit. So unintentionally, a father can emotionally wear down his child, causing the child to give up. Or as mentioned in Colossians, such consistent negative comments may cause our own flesh and blood to resent us. Dr. John Gottman, says, "For every negative comment we say to our or children, we must say between five to twenty positive comments to offset our one negative comment." Proverbs 18:21 reads, "The tongue has the power of life and death." Our words will either encourage or discourage our children.

The Bible urges fathers to be active parents. It also urges fathers to lead the spiritual development of their children. Fathers often think it is the mother's job to take the children to church, but this is a shared responsibility between both parents. To be successful in this, we are to be a "safe person" who is *approachable* for our children as we read about the characteristics of a godly father found in First Thessalonians 2:11-12. We have to do things that will make a positive impression on our children. We must encourage, comfort, display humility when we make mistakes, and show kindness to our children as Christ has shown that kindness to us. We cannot teach one thing and do another because that confuses our children and sends them mixed messages. Sometimes, our actions are so loud our children can't hear a word we are saying.

Fathers are responsible for teaching their children about their faith in God. Note that I said this is the *father's* job, not the church's job. Dads, don't just drop your kids off at church or send them off on the church bus every Sunday, expecting the church to teach the lessons you're supposed to be teaching. The church's job is only to supplement and support what is being taught at home.

Implementing this biblical blueprint should begin at pregnancy, if possible. Some couples sing Christian songs to their babies while they are in the womb. Others sing and read favorite Bible stories to their unborn children. These activities increase babies' ability to learn at an early age. Both of these activities seem to tremendously impact the children academically and spiritually, once he or she is born.

Researchers with *FamilyLife Today* say that the average father only spends fifteen minutes a day with his children. God commands fathers to teach their children, but how is that possible when such a small amount of time is spent with them? God-honoring fathers should strive to interact with their children using all aspects of life, teaching them spiritual truths to guide them for the rest of their lives.

Years ago, a program on MTV stated that teenagers in America who didn't work reportedly received approximately $100 million in combined allowances from their parents. These teenagers called this money "guilt money." Teenagers will spend whatever money we give to them, but these particular teenagers said they would rather have less money and more time with their parents. Fathers, you have a greater influence than you think and money can't always replace your time with your kids.

CHRISTIAN FATHERS ARE LISTENERS

*Fathering demands much wisdom. It requires wisdom to know when to be **tough** and when to be **tender**. You have to know what situation calls for toughness and firmness and when tenderness and gentleness are needed. It is easy to stay one speed, but being a balanced father demands shifting from one to the other. If a father is primarily **tough**, kids grow to be angry and discouraged. If a father is primarily **tender**, kids may never learn proper boundaries and consequences for their choices. Also, much of fathering is simply being there. Being available to talk and mostly listen.*

Dr. Johnny Parker, Pastor of Men's Ministry
First Baptist Church of Glenarden, MD

FATHERS ARE SENSITIVE

Fathers are to interact with sensitivity and caring, which doesn't translate into a man being weak. Fathers must model good behaviors in order to effectively interact with their children. We must first be effective listeners, which require patience and a "this isn't about me" attitude. When we interact with our children, we must give them our undivided attention.

I have always tried my best to give my daughters my full attention when they're talking to me. One of my daughters can be particularly long-winded, but I still listen to her when she has something to say. Now that two of them are away in college, they call or Skype me frequently to discuss boys, school, major decisions, their future, etc., in that order. As a father, it is priceless to have them call just to chat with me, or for them to ask me to drive two hours just to see them. Bottom line: invest in their lives now and they will always want you involved in their lives. This investment has provided peace of mind for me and trust about the kind of life they are living away from home.

Sometimes we need our wives' help to hear when our children are calling for our attention. This also goes for our wives helping us to hear when our children need us. Michelle, my middle daughter, was a very good basketball player. One day, she decided to stop playing basketball so she could learn how to play tennis instead. I was completely perplexed by her decision as I was hoping to get her a basketball scholarship and had dreams of her playing in the WNBA some day. Well, my wife saw it in a completely different way and told me, "With tennis, she has you all to herself."

I should have realized this years earlier. Michelle's other two sisters, Christina and Andrea, have always been aggressive for what they want. When they were younger, this included holding my hand whenever we went for walks. Michelle never fought or rushed to grab my hand so I assumed it was no big deal for her. That was until one day, when she was nine years old, and it was just the two of us. To my amazement, Michelle grabs my hand; causing me to realize that I need to give each of my three girls individual time with me. The good news is it is seldom too late to correct mistakes with our children, even when they become adults, because they so desperately want and need their father's love.

FATHERS STAND IN THE GAP

Real men don't leave their children because they realize how irreplaceable they are in the lives of their children. Jeff has already mentioned that it is more beneficial for children to have a residential father. Additionally, the African-American Healthy Marriage Initiative research reveals that children with residential fathers do better in every aspect of life, and that having a father in the home also helps the family do better financially. All of this helps the family to have a healthy legacy, positively influencing future generations. Seeing how much my dad loved my mom gave me such security and peace as a child, and the fact that they stayed together until death kept me from considering divorce as an option throughout my marriage.

Jeff's research has proven the positive influence of residential fathers as well as the negative results of absentee fathers.

ALTERNATIVE FATHERS ARE NEEDED

Our reality is that not all fathers ever were, or are always, residential fathers. So there is a serious need for alternative fathers. I'm so concerned about the need for children of single moms who need a good man in their lives that I strongly endorse alternative fathers.

Blended family or step family; neither term is used in the Bible, yet the Bible has a number of examples of blended families, providing ideas as to how these family situations might be successful and pleasing in God's sight. One biblical example of a step-father type is Jethro with Moses. Moses passes on what he learns from Jethro to Joshua. Moses prepares Joshua to lead approximately two million people to the Promised Land. Another well-known biblical example is the Apostle Paul helping a young boy who is raised by his mother and grandmother. Paul helps this insecure and timid young man to overcome these obstacles to become a leader. He also teaches Timothy to not allow his youth to be used by others as a detriment to him or the things he has been called to do.

While pastoring Freedom Baptist Church in Tulsa, Oklahoma, I asked single mothers if they would allow some of the men in the church to give hugs to their children. (Now, we put measures, such as background checks, in place to protect the children.) This enriched the lives of these children, their mothers, and the men in our church. Also, there were couples who couldn't have children that were so fulfilled by having this opportunity. Not only was this beneficial to the children and families involved, but this bonding experience also strengthened our church family. Our church was cross-cultural, so every Sunday you would see men and children of different cultures hugging each other.

The previous chapter mentions the incredible and invaluable influence that my alternative dads have played in my life as a single man, married man, and as a father. We all need the help and guidance of older men with integrity and godly character. Consider your legacy as it doesn't end just with your children. Be a mentor for other children as well. Your value to mankind might come to fruition with another man's child. We never know God's intention for our lives, nor do we know how He intends to use us for His glory. Your being a man and standing in the gap could be a life-changing aspect of your Christian walk.

CHRISTIAN FATHERS DISCIPLINE THEIR CHILDREN

"He must be one who manages his own household well, keeping his children under control with all dignity." 1Timothy 3:4

This verse reveals that we are to keep our children under control, meaning our children should be well-behaved at home and in public. Saving parents from embarrassing moments isn't the primary purpose of this verse, but teaching a child to be well-behaved all the time and helping the child learn self-control. Fathers are primarily responsible for applying this discipline. In no way am I saying mothers can't nor shouldn't discipline, but all of the pressure of disciplining the children shouldn't be placed on her shoulders alone. For example, it can be extremely difficult for some mothers to discipline teenage boys alone.

Many mothers have confessed to me, "When I tell my children to do something, it takes me telling them three or four times before they move; but my husband tells them to do something just once and it's done!" Fathers are so helpful in disciplining their children and raising them to respect both parents and authority is paramount.

God expects fathers to discipline their children. Discipline is motivated by love with the idea of correction to assist the child to make better decisions when it comes to his or her behavior. Discipline isn't to be confused with punishment, which desires retribution, and not the child's best interest.

This correction is to help children hit their target of a healthy, productive and fulfilled life. Our discipline should be motivated by our love for our children. Proverbs 13:24 supports this truth by saying, *He who spares the rod hates his son (child), but he who loves him is careful to discipline him.* Proverbs 29:15 states, "*The rod of correction imparts wisdom, but a child left to himself disgraces his mother.*" Have you ever seen an out-of-control toddler whose parent was just begging him or her to behave? If the parent doesn't discipline that child, eventually, the state will, using our tax dollars to do so.

Proverbs 29:17 reads, *Discipline your son, and he will give you peace; he will bring delight to your soul.* Such a child gives his/her parents peace because he/she will be at peace with himself. According to 2 Timothy 2:25, other words for discipline are instruction, training, or nurture. In other words, it's imperative to train your child to learn his proper behavior function in various circumstances. Children who are disciplined sense the love of the person who disciplines them because kids really want and need boundaries. They can sense if you love them, but they will almost always push you as far as you will let them. Boundaries give them security, which they translate as love. Your children knows you love them, but they won't respect you if allow them to be in charge. Allowing your child to be in charge isn't natural, normal, or healthy for either of you.

Dads who travel, or who are often away from home, have to make some adjustments because while he is gone his wife becomes the primary disciplinarian. When dad returns from his trip, he has to be careful about jumping back into his role since it can upset the home chemistry with his wife and his children. He needs to touch base with his wife and his children each day while he is gone, if possible. The longer he is gone from the home, the more difficult it may be for him to transition back into the role of primary disciplinarian. You will need to talk with the mother to make this transition work.

Another issue is that fathers need to support their wives when disciplining their children. Don't let your children divide your wife and you on disciplinary issues, instead, have a united front when dealing with your children. Don't be surprised if they try to play the two of you against each other. Don't get played! This is especially critical in co-parenting relationships when the parents aren't in a romantic relationship. Whatever your situation, a united front must be presented to the child.

Another benefit of discipline is found in Proverbs 13:18. This verse talks about avoiding poverty and shame, but instead, gaining honor.

Proverbs 12:1 says, *"Whoever loves discipline loves knowledge, but he who hates correction is stupid."* So we fathers are to be discipline and to teach discipline to our children. One of our fathering goals is found in Proverbs 13:1, *A wise son heeds his father's instruction, but a mocker does not listen to rebuke (strong correction).*

Hebrews 12:5-11 of the New Testament sheds more insight of God's perspective of discipline:

"And you have forgotten that word of encouragement that addresses you as sons: "My son, do not make light of the Lord's discipline, and do not lose heart when He rebukes you, because the Lord disciplines those he loves, and he punishes everyone he accepts as a son." Endure hardship as discipline; God is treating you as sons. For what son is not disciplined by his father? If you are not disciplined (and everyone undergoes discipline), then you are illegitimate children and not true sons. Moreover, we have all had human fathers who disciplined us and we respected them for it. How much more should we submit to the Father of our spirits and live! Our fathers disciplined us for a little while as they thought best; but God disciplines us for our good, that we may share in His holiness. No discipline seems pleasant at the time, but painful. Later on, however, it produces a harvest of righteousness and peace for those who have been trained by it."

This Hebrew passage is a gold mine filled with "fathering" nuggets. Let's get rich with these principles:

- God says that His discipline is a sign of love, so as fathers, our motivation for disciplining our children is our love for them, not to hurt or punish them.

- God says His discipline helps our spiritual development, which should be our motivation as fathers as well.

- God says a lack of discipline is a characteristic of a non-father—and the child feels unloved with no boundaries

- God says what we already know, which is that no discipline is pleasant at the time; but discipline produces peace. Peace is what so many of our youth of today don't have, resulting in so much violence by our youth. Youth workers have told me that many of our boys and girls have rage because their fathers are absent. This peace will allow our children to develop personal security and a balance of self-worth, not self-worship.

- If we train or discipline our children, according to research, there is an excellent chance that our children will pass this on to their children, who will experience this peace as a way of life.

- God says that fathers using discipline motivated by love, create respect for these fathers in the hearts of their children. In our society today, so many of our youth and young adults are willing to go to jail or even die for "respect." Disrespect, as they call it, isn't acceptable. Can you imagine raising a generation of youth who respect their fathers? This is the way our society used to be. Maybe there *are* some biblical principles that are beneficial for our family and society.

We fathers discipline our children as best we see fit, according to this Hebrew passage. What this passage is making us aware of is that none of us are perfect, so no one fathers perfectly; even though we would like to. What do we do when we mess up as a father? Ask our children for forgiveness and work at being better and more consistent, not perfect.

CHRISTIAN FATHERS PROVIDE DIRECTION & INFLUENCE

"Give your children direction, so they can have options later."
Charmas Lee, *Speed T& F,* Track & Fitness Consultant

Proverbs 22:6 teaches fathers to be proactive in their child's life at an early age. But there is another principle in this verse that needs close examination.

The phrase of this verse which says, *Train a child in a way he should go*, is actually translated "according to his or her bent—personality and stage of growth." This requires fathers becoming a student of their children in order to know *how* to train them. If your child has some artistic talent, help him in that area. Sports are easy—but this training must be for your child, not for you to live vicariously through your child. It requires a father to understand his child's actions and communications. He must know what motivates his kids, their emotions, and how they think. One way to *learn* your children is through praying with each one, individually. Children pray about what is most urgent to them, and by praying with our children individually, they will tell us how to parent them. Also, by praying with them each night, we create a safe place for them to share their victories, dreams, failures, and their fears. What a gift a father can give to his children; his time.

Abraham's character provides a biblical role model for us as he and his son Isaac walked together on a journey, according to Genesis 22:3-5, 8. The moral of this story of Abraham and Isaac is that Abraham spent time with his child, benefiting his son. In turn, Isaac trusted Abraham, his father with his life.

If we effectively spend time with our children, they'll actually teach us how to father them. They will let us know their dreams, victories, fears, and failures by sharing with us what's on their hearts. But this only occurs with quantity time. Quality time only comes out of *quantity time*!

Fathers … instead, bring them (your children) up in the training and instruction of the Lord, Ephesians 6:4 states. We are instructed to teach our children about God, which doesn't have to be a daily, intense one- to three-hour Bible study. A ten- to twenty-minute study, once or twice a week with your children would be beneficial to them and to you. I do this with my kids because I've seen the benefits. Sometimes with our hectic schedules, this can be tough, but teaching your children about God can fit into our daily routines as we drive to school or as life happens right before your eyes. Consider using the "What would Jesus Do?" principle for living life. To do this, a father interacts and if needed, intervenes regarding how his children are treating their mother, siblings, other children, school, etc., which will probably accumulate to more than fifteen minutes per day. This is good because God is expecting fathers to spend more than fifteen minutes a day with his children!

Fathers, during this time, you are laying the foundation for your children when they become adults. This foundation will support the spiritual formation of their lives. Often, it is easier for us to help strangers because they do not know us and our various (and numerous) quirks. However, you can give your children valuable help as a father by showing them your own shortcomings in life and how good God's grace is. Sharing our shortcomings and weaknesses serves as a wonderful opportunity to instruct and encourage our children by reminding them of how far we have come. Also, sharing our shortcomings and our life stories can help fill in the holes in the lives of those children we come in contact with who have been raised without their fathers. In telling our life story, we allow children to see our *"soft"* and human side and it helps them to not repeat our mistakes.

FATHERING ADULTS

The Bible gives an abundance of examples of how fathers relate to their adult children. These examples may give us a glimpse into how we might please God in our relationships with our adult children. This is good because they will likely seek our advice for their own relationships and family matters.

Jeff's research has already revealed the incredible positive influence of a man involved in the life of his child. This supports what I like to tell people, "Women have the amazing privilege of carrying life inside their bodies and men have the awesome privilege and responsibility of shaping life outside of the womb." A dear Christian female friend of mine in Atlanta once made a statement regarding fatherhood, which I've never been able to forget. She said, "A girl never overcomes the loss of her father." Whether her father walked away from her family, or if her parents divorced wasn't clear, but at some point he ceased having a role in her life. Her promiscuous lifestyle was a result of her looking for a man's love in the wrong places. She relates her past directly to not having a godly father in her home.

"Fathering is not difficult if you are an active father. I thought I had it easy by being a workaholic and giving my daughters anything they wanted. Now that they are grown and they have expressed their desire to spend more time with me, I regret being absent in their lives. If I could rewind time, I would have chosen the more difficult path of being there for them, to help them with homework, to put band-aids on their cuts, and the inevitable boy problems.

Fathering is easy if you give your children your undivided attention and unconditional love. My daughters and I took a road trip to visit my parents in Los Angeles not too long ago, and we spent the entire time talking about my childhood. They asked me all kinds of questions that I never knew they were interested in learning about. When we came home, they told their mom what a great time they had and how much they appreciated learning things about their father. Who would have thought what a rewarding experience it could be to just to be there in the moment and spend quality time with your children" Angel Maniego, a father of adult children from California. **Angel shows us that it is never too late to become a good father!**

Godly Fathers Financially Provide for Their Families

Jeff also mentioned earlier that men often feel their primary responsibility as fathers is to financially provide for their children. This is a core value for a man. First Timothy 5:8 reads, *If anyone (referring to a man because in the time & culture this book was written, few women could support a family) does not provide for his relatives, and especially his immediate family, he has denied the faith and is worse than an unbeliever.* Some translations call a man who doesn't provide for his family a fool or an infidel. Psalm 17:14 speaks of men leaving their fortune to their babies. So providing for our family is critical for a man, but fathering requires so much more than providing for one's family financially, and today this is no small task.

Providing for my family is constantly on my mind but God has *never* failed to provide for us!

What Will Your Legacy Be?

No matter what your job—whether garbage collector or president of a company—don't be ashamed of it because your children aren't ashamed of you, unless you give them a reason to be. No one can give your kids what you can give them, which is *you.* My dad was a janitor for thirty-eight years and he still is my hero. He worked three jobs for almost forty years to support our family. He demonstrated to me how to work hard.

A father is a teacher of life. When fathers don't teach their children about their own personal lives, children grow up with gaps, which they have difficulty in filling. Without having these "father-gaps" filled, some children never mature emotionally into balanced and well-adjusted adults.

My dad is in heaven now and in some ways, I've never recovered from his death. I've adopted other dads and grandfathers who have taught me important life lessons, but I still would have loved having him to teach me, in his terms, what it means to be a man.

In Numbers 14:18, the Bible says that the sins of the father will impact his family to the third and fourth generations. The Bible reveals a principle to us that secular research has since discovered. According to the Bible, fathers do positively or negatively impact not just our children, but our grandchildren and possibly even our great-grandchildren. What we as fathers do with our children has long term consequences! The character of a dad has a lasting influence on his children. Are you getting the point?

I can't tell you how excited I was when Brenda said, "I'm pregnant with twins!" My manhood filled the room! As my girls get older, I'm learning that fathering is a lifelong job with tremendous consequences and great rewards. Two are away in college, yet they say they still want and need me in their lives. But how can we be sure that we are doing a good job? With the Bible, we have been provided with a wealth of knowledge and practical examples; but just having the information won't make us good or better fathers. We have to put the principles into practice. What helps me to be sensitive to my wife and to my daughters, is the indwelling power of the Holy Spirit. I'm banking on God's grace to cover my mistakes. Fathering for me is a work in progress.

Do you want help with your fathering? Have a personal relationship with Jesus Christ. If you want to know more about Jesus Christ or how to have a relationship with Him, then please carefully read this next section.

THE REAL DIFFERENCE MAKER FOR FATHERING

The real difference for me as a father is having a personal relationship with Jesus Christ. As a follower of Jesus Christ, God lives inside me through the Person of the Holy Spirit. The Holy Spirit empowers, encourages, teaches, and reminds Christian fathers of the things they should do for and with their children. Would you like to have the Holy Spirit living inside of you giving you the additional help you need to father your children and so that you are never alone?

Establishing a personal relationship with Jesus Christ is very easy and simple. First, it begins by believing that God created man (Adam & Eve) as the crowning achievement of all of His creation. Until Adam and Eve disobeyed God they had perfect fellowship with God. The consequence of their sin was death, but God didn't kill them. Instead, he banished them from the Garden of Eden. God sent His only Son, Jesus Christ, who was fully God, who became man (and still be God simultaneously), and lived a sinless life, despite being tempted in every way. Then Jesus paid the penalty of sin by dying on the cross for every person's sin whether born or to be born, in the place of all mankind; you and me. Then God raised Jesus Christ from the dead on the third day to have victory over death. Now, you and I can have eternal life with Jesus Christ by simply asking Him to forgive us of our sin (we were born in sin because of Adam—father of all mankind) and to come into our lives and make it what He wants it to be. It is just that simple. It is an act of faith. If we are sincere, then God in the Person of the Holy Spirit will come live inside of us.

Read the following verses found in the book of Romans:

"Therefore, just as sin entered the world through one man, and death through sin, and in this way death came to all men, because all sinned." Romans 5:12

"There is none righteous, not even one." Romans 3:10

"For all have sinned and fall short of the glory of God." Romans 3:23

"But God demonstrates His love for us in this: While we were still sinners, Christ died for us." Romans 5:8

"For the wages of sin is death, but the gift of God is eternal life in Christ Jesus our Lord." Romans 6:23

"That if you confess with your mouth, 'Jesus is Lord," and believe in your heart that God raised Him (Jesus Christ) from the dead, you will be saved (rescued/delivered). For it is with your heart that you believe and are justified, and it is with your mouth that you confess (agree with God) and are saved." Romans 10:9-10

The words aren't magic, but if this is the **desire of your heart**, simply ask Jesus Christ to forgive you for your sins and to come into your life as your Lord and Savior right now, and He will. This act isn't based on emotions or feeling, but the truth of God's word.

Prayer for a Personal Relationship with Jesus Christ:

Lord Jesus, I need You. Thank You for dying on the cross for my sins. I admit that I am a sinner and I am separated from You. Please forgive me. I receive You as my Savior and Lord. Thank You for forgiving my sins and giving me eternal life. Please take control of my life. Make me the kind of person You want me to be. Amen.

Having Christ in your heart is what I truly believe to be the difference maker in fathering. Much of Jeff's research supports the principles of the Bible. To my knowledge, no one has written a book like this before. I hope you have found it helpful. Whether or not you believe, faith makes a difference in fathering. But I hope you do see the Bible has a wealth of knowledge for fathers. As fathers, we're all on the same team, trying to help our children experience the best life has to offer.

WHAT DO YOU THINK?

(Questions to answer for yourself, with your father if possible, in a small group, or with girlfriend/spouse)

- What is your impression of this chapter?

- What are you thinking about the possible influence of faith in your fathering efforts?

- What did you enjoy most, or find most beneficial, in this chapter?

- What difference to you think praying with your child at night before he or she goes to bed will make in their life? What about yours?

- What are some ways you can make your wife's, or the mother of your child's, life easier?

- What are some ways you are already nurturing your child or what ways can you begin nurturing your child?

- Would your child say that you are a good listener? Why or Why not?

- How are you giving your child direction so he or she can have options later?

- Before reading this chapter, have you thought how important the words you speak to your children are? Would they say you are an encourager or discourager? Why?

- Did you ask Jesus Christ to come into your life? Why or Why not?

CONCLUSION
CHAPTER 8

Over the past three years, this project has been a labor of love as I reminisce about my how girls have grown. Each day, I'm grateful that they are a part of my life and cherish the time we have spent together. This is especially true now that Jordan is 17 and beginning her senior year in high school. Her time residing with me is nearing an end, so I am really cherishing these last days before she leaves for college. Jiera is entering middle school and is as bright as can be. Her personality from childhood is the same. And just like her toddler days, she is always with me—we are still tied at the hip! We have such a close relationship. She proudly answers "Yes" whenever asked if she is a *Daddy's girl*. Nine year old Jadah is going to the 4th grade and is absolutely hilarious. Her strong personality and quick wit keeps all of us laughing. There aren't many people that can bring me to tears because they make me laugh so hard, but she can. Truly she is a comedian. I am not predicting this for her, but no one in our family would be surprised if she didn't make a career using her keen sense of humor.

Being a father has not become any easier than when I first got married and had my first child. As a matter of fact, it has become more challenging because it is more time consuming. Given that all my girls are involved in numerous extracurricular activities – I spend a good portion of my time taking them to practice, games, and attending their events. But I enjoy seeing them compete and being active just as much as they enjoy participating.

Much of what we do as fathers go unrecognized, but that is okay because our efforts are far more important than anyone could possibly give us credit for. Let me encourage you men to stay strong and involved in your efforts to raise your children. If there has been a disconnect with your child, there is always time to reconnect and make things right. Children tend to be very forgiving.

My motivation for writing this book was to empower men and educate society as to how essential we are in our fathering role. Secondly, I wanted to reach out to fathers to explain and encourage them to expand their roles as dads. I'm convinced that being exposed to someone else's fathering experiences may broaden our understanding, helping us to improve our own effectiveness as fathers. Finally, I wanted to give fathering a purpose and validation. The Bible is a rich source of stories of fathers, showing how their interactions with their children effected many subsequent generations. Through these examples, I wanted us to see how necessary we are generationally and how far our legacy extends past our immediate family. Hopefully, my sharing of my triumphs and failures as a father has been beneficial. Once we come to the understanding of our purpose and calling for our children it will help to put life in perspective.

As we become new fathers please remember that little ones need you also. Moms are going to want a lot of time with the new born, which is natural, so don't let that bother you. Get in time with your child when you can. Purposefully get some time alone with your little one. Hold him or her on your chest while you watch the game on TV or on the computer, which are excellent times to bond. Rescue them when they cry or are hungry or tired. A father's reassuring voice will help them to know that everything is "okay 'cause' daddy is here." As they get older, it becomes easier to have them with you more. Try to have them accompany you when you run errands or visit friends. My girls often accompany me and have gone so many places with me. As I play ball, officiate, or give a presentation I have them come with me to observe. I always promised them a treat if they would sit and stay where I could see them. Many times I had my 6 and 4 year olds in the gym with me as I played a pickup game of basketball. Since I had girls, it was like having my own cheering section. We live busy lives so try to include them in as much of your routine as you can. After your wife, if you are married, make them your priority.

As children age they continue to need your love, guidance, support, and reassurance. Life can seem tough for a child, but just as when they were little ones, daddies can make it better. Spend alone time with your children without their siblings some of the time *consistently*. I always kept my girls active and tried to make their practices and games. I have spent many hours throwing the ball back to my two older ones as they shot baskets in the drive way. I could have purchased one of those ball returns that you place on a basketball hoop, although it would return the ball to them, it would not replace my attention to them and time spent. This time with them allowed us to bond. It also expressed my love to them and gave them security. Reward good behaviors. Have high, but realistic expectations for your children. Help them with their school work and give them age appropriate responsibilities. One thing that I have learned is as you help your children set goals, for example with school, they don't always achieve them. I have recently been pointing out to Jiera why she got a "B" in math on her report card and not an "A" which was her goal. We have dialogued about things she needs to do to help her reach her goal. Her problem is turning in late assignments or missing assignments. So I help to educate her by showing her that the 88 grade in math was due to missed work as most of her graded assignments were 100s. "Why do you think you only got a B," I asked? She responded that she turned some assignments in late and missed one. We had discussed that she would get her own phone if she made all A's. I kept my end of the agreement, no phone! I know she can do the work; it is a matter of me making her responsible for meeting her goals and being rewarded for meeting it. Of course, she feels that she should still get a phone. But in life there are consequences for our actions or lack thereof; so now is a perfect time is now to teach her this principle.

My advice is to be very purposeful in your interactions with your children. Take the time to spend time and teach them as many life lessons as you can. Do it with love, compassion and reinforce positive behaviors as your children will be the better for it. Hopefully if these things are emphasized when they are children the transition to adolescent won't be so difficult.

My oldest is leaving in a year. I'll be rid of one teen-ager only to have another coming right behind her. Then in a couple of years, will have two teens in one house. Boy! But if things go as well as with Jordan, I should be able to handle it. With teenagers there are going to be some bumps in the road, learning curves, or disappointing moments. It comes with the territory! I may have been the only teen who didn't give my parents any trouble.

They may tell you different, but I am sticking with the story. Teenagers want to do all the adult stuff but don't want any of the responsibility. They want to clean their room when they want to i.e., when they want to go somewhere or have friends over. They want to stay out late, change their initial plan without informing you and do stuff on their own time frame. Then they turn around and ask you for the keys to the car you paid for, credit card to put in gas, and cash for dinner. I remember thinking, "Are you serious?" We just had this long drawn out conversation about why you haven't completed your chores, homework, what I asked you to do two days ago and the only reason you could come up with was I forgot, I was busy, it's still not done. Now, you have the audacity to take your car (that is in my name and under my insurance), get my gas card out of the kitchen drawer and ask me for money for the movies. Only a teenager would assume that they had the rights to these things and promise on the way out the door that they will take care of all their responsibilities when they get back home.

Sometimes, I just shake my head, pray for patience and other times I lose it. But losing it doesn't really work because perception is greater than reality. When you lose it, fuss, and react negatively, your children perceive you are trippin. Jordan says, "What's wrong with you why are you trippin or upset?" Then your mouth drops as you try to explain why you are upset. But it just doesn't seem to equate or make sense. Remember to them, their friends or their friends' parents are *doing it* or *can go* is all the rationale they need. Anything else is irrational in their minds. But this too shall pass and it is a good chance that your relationship will grow stronger with your children as they reach adulthood.

Being a father doesn't stop just because your children become adults, but your role probably does change. Most fathers become more like companions or friends with their adult children. Your children might still seek advice on some matters. It is crucial to serve the role in which your children are comfortable because you do not want to be offering advice when it is not wanted. But always let your adult children feel that you are approachable and are available when needed.

I continue to be amazed how much influence my father has on me even though I am in my mid 40's. We don't talk every day, but he will call me if he doesn't hear from me in a week or two to check to see how things are going. He is really cool about helping me with the girls if I have to travel and will go out of his way to be there for me. He has often told me how proud he is of my brother and me and that means the world to me!

Your role as father will be both trying and rewarding! Although this book will not make your role less trying or more rewarding, I hope that it helps you have a better understanding and appreciation of your role as dad. You are making a difference for a lifetime either positively or negatively as a dad! Remember, it is not about perfection, but consistency. You can do it!

WHAT ALL DADS SHOULD KNOW
DR. JEFFREY SHEARS
DR. CLARENCE SHULER

REFERENCES

Beatty, M. J., & Dobos, J. A. (1993). Adult males' perceptions of confirmation and relational partner communication apprehension: Indirect effects of fathers on sons' partners. *Communication Quarterly*, 41, 66-76.

Berry, P. (1990). *Fathers and Mothers.* Dallas, TX: Spring.

Buerkel-Rothfuss, N. L., & Yerby, J. (1981, October). Two studies in member perceptions of family communication: Part LP Perceived similarity in intergenerational communication style. Part 11: A factor analytic study of family communication patterns. Paper presented to National Council on Family Relations, Milwaukee, WI.

Conger, R. D., & Elder, G. H. (1994). *Families in troubled times. Adapting to change in rural America.* New York: Aldine de Gruyter.

Duncan, G.J., Hill, M., & Yeung, J. (1996). Fathers' activities and child attainments. Paper presented at the NICHD Family and Child Well-Being Network's Conference on Father Involvement, Bethesda, MD.

Hawkins, A. J., & Dollahite, D. C. (1997). Beyond the role-inadequacy perspective. In A. J. Hawkins & D. C. Dollahite (Eds.), *Generating fathering: Beyond deficit perspectives* (pp. 3-16). Thousand Oaks, CA: Sage.

Ellis, B. J., Bates, J. E., Dodge, K. A., Fergusson, D. M., Horwood, L. J., Pettit, G. S., et al. (2003). Does father absence place daughters at special risk for early sexual activity? *Child Development,74,* 801–822.

Farrell, A. D., & White, K. S. (1998). Peer influences and drug use among urban adolescents: Family structure and parent-adolescent relationship as protective factors. *Journal of Counseling and Clinical Psychology, 66,* 248–258.

Fink, D. S. (1993). *Father-son relationships: Relational closeness and fathers' parenting style as predictors of sons' expected parenting style and communicator style similarity.* Unpublished master's thesis. Central Michigan University, Mt. Pleasant.

Simons, R. L., Beaman, J., Conger, R., & Chao, W. (1993). Stress, support, and antisocial behavior trait as determinants of emotional well-being and parenting practices among single mothers. *Journal of Marriage and Family, 55,* 385–399.

Fisher, T. D. (1987). *Child sexual attitude similarity as a function of communication about sex and proximity.* (ERIC Document Reproduction Service No. ED 284 080).

Glenn & Kramer, (1987). The marriages and divorce of the children of divorce. *Journal of Marriage and the family, 49,* 811-825.

Harris, K. M., Furstenberg, F. F. Jr., and Marmer, J.K. (1998). Paternal involvement with adolescents in intact families: The influence of fathers over the life course." *Demography 35*:201-16.

Harper, C. C., & McLanahan, S. S. (2004). Father absence and youth incarceration. *Journal of Research on Adolescence, 14,* 369-397.

Hawkins & Dollahite, 1997 Palkovitz, R. (1997) 'Reconstructing "involvement": expanding conceptualizations of men's caring in contemporary families', in A. J. Hawkins and D. C. Dollahite (eds) *Generative Fathering: Beyond Deficit Perspectives*, pp. 200–16. Thousand Oaks, CA: SAGE.

Lamb, M. E., & Lamb, J. E.(1976). The nature and importance of the father infant relationship. *Family Coordinator, 25,* 379–386.

Lamb,M. E. (1997). *The role of the father in child development* (3rd ed.). New York: Wiley.

Lamb, M. E. (2000). The history of research on father involvement: An overview. *Marriage & Family Review, 29,* 23–42.

Lykken, D. T. (1997). Factory of crime. *Psychological Inquiry, 8,* 261-270.;

Marsiglio,W., Day, R., & Lamb, M. E. (2000). Exploring fatherhood diversity: Implications for conceptualizing father involvement. *Marriage and Family Review, 29,* 269–293.

Marsiglio,W., Hutchinson, S., & Cohan, M. (2000). Envisioning fatherhood: A social psychological perspective on young men without kids. *Family Relations, 49,* 133–142.

McLanahan, S., & Sandefur, S. (1994). *Growing up with a single parent: What hurts, what helps.* Cambridge, MA: Harvard University Press.

Nielsen, L. (2001) Fathers and Daughters: Why a course for college students? *College Student Journal, 35,*280-316.

Singer, A.T.B., & Weinstein, R.S. (2000). Differential parental treatment predicts achievement and self-perceptions in two cultural contexts. *Journal of Family Psychology, 14,* 491–509.

Simons, R.L., Beaman J, Conger, R.D., Chao W. (1993). Childhood experience, conceptions of parenting, and attitudes of spouse as determinants of parental behavior. *Journal of Marriage and Family, 55,* 91–106.

Simons, R. L., Johnson, C., & Conger, R. D. (1994). Harsh Corporal Punishment Versus quality of Parental Involvement as an Explanation of Adolescent Maladjustment. *Journal of Marriage and the Family,* 56, 591-607.

Simons R.L., Whitbeck, L.B., Conger, R.D., Wu, C. (1991). Intergenerational transmission of harsh parenting. *Developmental Psychology, 27,* 159–171.

Snarey, J. (1993). *How fathers care for the next generation.* Cambridge, MA: Harvard University Press.

Spruijt, E., Degoede, M., & Vandervalk, I. (2001). The well-being of youngsters coming from six different family types. *Patient Education and Counseling, 45,* 285–94.

Yogman, M. (1981). Games fathers and mothers play with their infants. *Infant Mental Health Journal, 2,* 241–248.

WHAT ALL DADS SHOULD KNOW
DR. JEFFREY SHEARS
DR. CLARENCE SHULER

MEET THE AUTHORS

DR. JEFFREY K. SHEARS

Dr. Jeffrey K. Shears is an Associate Professor, Director of the Social Work Research Consortium, and BSW Coordinator in the Department of Social Work at UNC-Charlotte. Professor Shears, a National Early Head Start Research and Evaluation Consortium Member, has served as Director of Fathers' Study in Denver, CO. He earned his Bachelor's degree in Social Work, M.ED in Education Administration from North Carolina A&T State University and Ph.D. in Social Work from the University of Denver.

Presently, he teaches an undergraduate and graduate level Research Methods course which focuses on research designs, program evaluation, and intermediate statistical analyses. Professor Shears' research interests include fathering, juvenile delinquency, multicultural issues, particularly those effecting students in higher education. Some of his recent publications are *Fathering Attitudes and Practices: Influences on Children's Development; Interpersonal Relationships as Predictors of Delinquency across Ethnic and Racial Sample; Exploring Fathering Roles in Low-Income Families; The influence of Intergenerational Transmission; and School Bonding as a Protective Factor Against Drug Use in Rural Youth.*

His national and international publications are in numerous respected refereed journals which include; Families in Society; Social Work Research, Advances in Social Work, Infant Mental Health Journal, and Parenting: Science and Practice. He also has co-authored a book chapter in the widely used *Social Work: A profession of many faces.* Professor Shears has appeared in the APA monitor, *The Charlotte Post, The Denver Post,* and on the *Northern Colorado Public Broadcast Network.*

Dr. Clarence Shuler

Dr. Shuler is husband to Brenda, father to 3 female college students (he's the minority in their sorority), author, marriage counselor, speaker, and life & relationship coach. Clarence is President/CEO of *BLR: Building Lasting Relationships*. For over 25 years, Brenda and he have conducted marriage, men's, women's, and singles' seminars (United States & internationally). They're members of *FamilyLife's* Weekend To Remember Marriage Speaker Team. They've taught Managing Marriage/Family & Ministry for The Billy Graham Schools of Evangelism. He assists the U.S. Department of Health & Human Services (Administration for Children & Families) in its National African American Healthy Marriage Initiative. He's a certified Marriage Educator. They also help military marriages, especially in the area of overcoming affairs and surviving deployment.

As a Life & Relationship Coach, Clarence helps executives experience fulfillment in their personal/professional lives. He's been featured several times in *Essence Magazine, Discipleship Journal, Black Enterprise* and other magazines as well as radio. He's authored six books, including *Keeping Your Wife Your Best Friend. Winning the Race to Unity* is used by colleges/graduate schools as a textbook, inspiring Wheaton College's first ever *Civil Rights Movement Conference!* A few of his diversity clients: War College of U.S. Air Force, U.S. Army Equal Opportunity Advisors (Europe), Mississippi Valley State University, plus numerous churches, Christian universities & organizations. Clarence is a member of the Coalition for Black Marriages/Families. *Winning the Race to Unity* is also a resource for the 2011 diversity movie, *The GraceCard.*

Healthy Family Seminar Mission Statement:

The Healthy Family Seminar provides effective tools and resources to help improve family relationships, specifically in the areas of fathering, marriage (relationships), and the maltreatment of children & adults in relaxed and interactive sessions.

Healthy Family Seminar Description:

Healthy Families Seminar is an affordable, fun, informative, interactive and life-changing one-day (6 hour) seminar. As a one-day seminar is not designed to be an exhaustive seminar. One goal of this seminar is developing an ongoing relationship in which more aspects of fathering, marriage (relationships), and the maltreatment of children will be addressed in future seminars (possibly 3-4 Healthy Families Seminars yearly for a church or organization).

179

WHAT ALL DADS SHOULD KNOW
DR. JEFFREY SHEARS
DR. CLARENCE SHULER

HealthyFamily

"Helping Families Improve & Maintain Their Health"
HealthyFamily Publishing

Contact :
Dr. Shears at jkshears@uncc.edu
Dr. Shuler at clarencefs@gmail.com
(719) 282-1340
www.HealthyFamilySeminar.com

WHAT ALL DADS SHOULD KNOW
DR. JEFFREY SHEARS
DR. CLARENCE SHULER